Commonly Misunderstood Verses of the Bible

Commonly Misunderstood Verses of the Bible

What They Really Mean

ROBERT E. VAN VOORST

CASCADE *Books* · Eugene, Oregon

COMMONLY MISUNDERSTOOD VERSES OF THE BIBLE
What They Really Mean

Copyright © 2017 Robert E. Van Voorst. All rights reserved. Except for brief quotations in critical publications or reviews, no part of this book may be reproduced in any manner without prior written permission from the publisher. Write: Permissions, Wipf and Stock Publishers, 199 W. 8th Ave., Suite 3, Eugene, OR 97401.

Cascade Books
An Imprint of Wipf and Stock Publishers
199 W. 8th Ave., Suite 3
Eugene, OR 97401

www.wipfandstock.com

PAPERBACK ISBN: 978-1-5326-1027-1
HARDCOVER ISBN: 978-1-5326-1029-5
EBOOK ISBN: 978-1-5326-1028-8

Cataloguing-in-Publication data:

Names: Van Voorst, Robert E., author.
Title: Commonly misunderstood verses of the Bible : what they really mean / Robert E. Van Voorst.
Description: Eugene, OR: Cascade Books, 2017 | Includes bibliographical references.
Identifiers: ISBN 978-1-5326-1027-1 (paperback) | ISBN 978-1-5326-1029-5 (hardcover) | ISBN 978-1-5326-1028-8 (ebook).
Subjects: LCSH: Bible—Criticism, interpretation, etc.
Classification: BS511.3 V36. 2017 (print) | BS511.3 (ebook).

Manufactured in the U.S.A.

Unless otherwise noted, all Scripture quotations are taken from the New Revised Standard Version Bible, copyright © 1989, Division of Christian Education of the National Council of the Churches of Christ in the United States of America. Used by permission. All rights reserved.
Scripture quotations marked (RSV) are taken from the Revised Standard Version of the Bible, copyright © 1946, 1952, and 1971 National Council of the Churches of Christ in the United States of America. Used by permission. All rights reserved.
Scripture quotations marked (NIV) are taken from the Holy Bible, New International Version®, NIV®. Copyright © 1973, 1978, 1984, 2011 by Biblica, Inc.™ Used by permission of Zondervan. All rights reserved worldwide. www.zondervan.com. The "NIV" and "New International Version" are trademarks registered in the United States Patent and Trademark Office by Biblica, Inc.™

With Gratitude to the Churches Where I Received or Gave the
Ministry of the Word:
Maplewood Reformed Church, Holland, Michigan
Rochester Reformed Church, Accord, New York
Lycoming Presbyterian Church, Williamsport, Pennsylvania
St. Ebbe's Church, Oxford, England
Third Reformed Church, Holland, Michigan

Preface

BIBLICAL ILLITERACY IS A widely recognized problem in Protestant churches, both mainline and evangelical. Adult North American Christians don't know the Bible as well as their parents and grandparents did. What is more, sometimes they "know" things about it that aren't true because they misunderstand key Bible verses, some of which are their favorite verses. Not everyone misunderstands these verses, of course, and most verses that appeal to Christians are not misconstrued. But misunderstandings happen often enough, and with passages important enough, to have a significant negative impact on the life of individual Christians, on the church, and at times even on the wider culture. A correction of these misunderstandings would, I believe, be a valuable contribution to the church. This is what I work toward in *Commonly Misunderstood Verses of the Bible: What They Really Mean*.

This book begins with an introduction on how and why Bible verses are misunderstood so often, which will also briefly introduce many of the twenty-four misunderstandings treated later. I also offer suggestions on how to read the Bible more carefully. The sections on the misunderstood verses are structured as follows: Each section opens with a quotation of the misunderstood verse. Then comes a statement, with illustrations from contemporary life, of the misunderstanding of this verse. This is followed by an explanation of the correct meaning of the verse, usually in a succinct close reading of the passage where the verse is found. Then I give a concise statement of how the misunderstanding may be partially correct or otherwise have some value. Finally, I relate the corrected meaning of the verse to Christian life today, and show that this new meaning offers something significant. Each section closes with questions for reflection and discussion that can be used by groups or individuals.

Finally, I want to address a direct, personal word to my readers. In my three years of speaking on this topic in various churches and teaching an online course on it, I have become aware of the powerful appeal many of these verses have for you. It may be unsettling for you, both emotionally and spiritually, to think that this appeal might be based at least in part on a misunderstanding. I want to thank you for "bearing with me" by considering this treatment of these verses. I encourage you to think it through, carefully and prayerfully, and reach your own conclusions on them. My hope is that the new meanings offered here may appeal to you, and come to be significant in your faith and life.

Acknowledgments

AN EARLIER VERSION OF this book has been used in churches through Journey, the continuing- and church-education department of Western Theological Seminary in Holland, Michigan, where I teach. Treatment of twelve misunderstood verses was offered in an online course in 2014. Twenty churches signed up to use it in Sunday classes, in Bible study groups, or in other settings, and gave me good feedback for the revision and improvement of this project. I want to thank the staff of Journey, especially Tara Macias, Pam Bush, and Keith Derrick, for their considerable help in this Journey course.

I completed this book while on sabbatical in the fall semester of 2016. I thank the administration of Western Theological Seminary for providing this sabbatical. My thanks also extend to Pam Bush for so helpfully reviewing and critiquing the final form of the manuscript, and to my academic dean, Alvin Padilla, for providing the funds to make this possible.

I thank the staff of Cascade Books for taking on this project. Dr. K. C. Hanson and his staff did excellent work in the production of this book.

Finally, I should express my thanks to the members of my family for their love and support: Mary, my wife, who inspires me by her devotion to the Christian faith; our son Richard and his wife, Bonnie, with their children William, Robert, and Camille; and our son Nicholas and his wife, Jessica, with their daughter, Octavia.

Contents

Preface | vii

Acknowledgments | ix

Introduction | 1

1. What Is the Mark of Cain? | 11

"And the Lord put a mark on Cain, so that no one who came upon him would kill him" (Genesis 4:15).

2. Is "Mizpah" a Benediction? | 17

"Therefore the name of it was called . . . Mizpah; for Laban said, "The Lord watch between me and thee, when we are absent one from another" (Genesis 31:48–49, KJV).

3. What Killing Does God Forbid? | 22

"You shall not kill" (Exodus 20:13).

4. Is "An Eye for an Eye" Vengeance? | 29

"If any harm follows, then you shall give life for life, eye for eye, tooth for tooth, hand for hand, foot for foot, burn for burn, wound for wound, stripe for stripe" (Exodus 21:23–25).

5. How Prosperous Does God Want Us to Be? | 34

"Then you shall make your way prosperous, and then you shall have good success" (Joshua 1:8).

6. How Do We Hide God's Word in Our Hearts? | 40

"I have hidden your word in my heart that I might not sin against you" (Psalm 119:11, NIV).

7. Is "Train up a Child" a Promise? | 45

"Train up a child in the way he should go, and when he is old he will not depart from it" (Proverbs 22:6).

8. The End of the World or the Beginning of a New World? | 51

"For I am about to create new heavens and a new earth" (Isaiah 65:17).

9. What Plans Does God Have for Us? | 58

"For I know the plans I have for you, says the Lord, plans to prosper you and not to harm you, plans to give you hope and a future" (Jeremiah 29:11).

10. Should Christians Forgive and Forget? | 63

"I will forgive their iniquity, and remember their sin no more" (Jeremiah 31:34).

11. Was Jesus Born in a Manger? | 69

"And she gave birth to her firstborn son and wrapped him in bands of cloth, and laid him in a manger, because there was no place for them in the inn" (Luke 2:7).

12. Don't Judge at All? | 75

"Judge not, that you be not judged" (Matthew 7:1).

13. If We Ask, Will We Really Receive? | 81

"Ask, and it will be given to you; search, and you will find; knock, and the door will be opened for you" (Matthew 7:7).

14. Who Are "the Least of These"? | 87

"Truly I tell you, just as you did it to one of the least of these brothers and sisters of mine, you did it to me" (Matthew 25:40).

15. What Cross Must We Bear? | 93

"If anyone wants to follow me, let him deny himself, take up his cross and follow me" (Mark 8:34).

16. Is "The Poor You Have with You Always" a Directive? | 98
"The poor you have with you always" (Mark 14:7).

17. Who Is a Good Samaritan? | 103
"But a Samaritan while traveling came near him; and when he saw him, he was moved with pity. He went to him, poured oil and wine on his wounds, and bandaged them. Then he put him on his own animal, brought him to an inn, and took care of him" (Luke 10:33–34).

18. How Did God Give His Only Son? | 108
"For God so loved the world that he gave his only Son, so that everyone who believes in him may not perish but may have eternal life" (John 3:16).

19. Should We Have All Possessions in Common? | 113
"All who believed were together and had all things in common" (Acts 2:44).

20. How Do All Things Work Together for Good? | 119
"We know that all things work together for good for those who love God" (Romans 8:28).

21. Will God Give Us More than We Can Bear? | 125
"God is faithful, and he will not let you be tested beyond your strength" (1 Corinthians 10:13).

22. What Things Can I Do in Christ? | 131
"I can do all things through him who strengthens me" (Philippians 4:13).

23. What Is the Root of All Evil? | 136
"For the love of money is the root of all evil" (1 Timothy 6:10).

24. Why Is Jesus Knocking at the Door? | 141
"Behold, I stand at the door and knock. If anyone hears my voice and opens the door, I will come in to him and eat with him, and he with me" (Revelation 3:20).

Bibliography | 147

Introduction

BEFORE WE DEAL DIRECTLY with the commonly misunderstood verses of the Bible, we should examine briefly the wider topic of understanding and misunderstanding the Bible. First, we will discuss why misunderstandings occur and why they have become so common. Next, we will consider questions people ask about the topic of commonly misunderstood verses. Finally, several suggestions will be offered on how to read the Bible in order to understand it more carefully.

WHY ARE SOME VERSES OF THE BIBLE MISUNDERSTOOD?

Some of the verses examined in this book are so widely misunderstood that we might think that their correct meaning is largely unknown. People can refer to the "mark of Cain" as a punishment, or say, "Money is the root of all evil," and others will easily nod their heads in agreement. Other verses examined here are known a bit more carefully than these two, but are still misinterpreted by many. No single reason explains all these misunderstandings. Here are the main factors that contribute to this problem.

1. Taking a verse out of its literary context in its passage is probably the leading cause of misunderstandings. Reading a verse while ignoring its surrounding verses can more readily make that verse say something we want it to mean but that the author didn't. This is usually done to meet the felt spiritual needs of the readers. An old motto in biblical interpretation says, "A text without a context is a pretext," and the pretext is often for reading what one wants to be there, not what God is really saying through the human authors of the Bible. For example, Jesus' statement "the poor are with you always" (Mark 14:7) is

quoted but the second half of it, "and you always have opportunity to help them" is left off, a tampering with this verse that enables the first part to be used to discourage Christians or governments from helping the poor. This goes against the full statement by Jesus, and it also contradicts the passage in Deuteronomy that Jesus draws on, which commands God's people in the strongest terms to help the poor.

2. Reading out of context is at times enabled by a notion that each verse of the Bible is inspired on its own and can be used on its own. This can lead to distortion of meaning. For example, when Jeremiah 29:11, "For I know the plans I have for you," declares the LORD, "plans to prosper you and not to harm you, plans to give you hope and a future" (NIV) is read by itself and applied to individuals today, its meaning gets twisted. Each verse is shaped by the verses that surround it, and cannot be understood in isolation. No Christian denomination has a doctrine of biblical inspiration which states that individual verses *on their own* are authoritative. Christians typically hold that the Bible is inspired in a way that makes it the Word of God for us, but to think that each verse of the Bible (or even a part of a verse such as "an eye for an eye" or "judge not") is fully inspired, and can operate on its own in the Christian life, is to embrace what I call overinspiration.

3. Memorizing single verses without regard to their context can lead to trouble. A widespread practice in Bible memorization is to memorize single verses or sentences. This probably came from Christian education of young children in Protestant churches, where it was thought that memorizing single, short verses was most effective educationally. Memorization fell on hard times in mainline Protestant church education from the 1960s through the 1980s, but at present it is making a comeback. Now there is a commendable emphasis on learning a few continuous verses in a passage, even though this cannot be expected of children and might also be a challenge for some teenagers and adults. (Those who choose a "life verse" as their main biblical inspiration should definitely learn the passage in which it appears.) Many evangelical churches, on the other hand, never gave up the practice of learning single verses, and parachurch organizations engaged in evangelism have long stressed the value of learning single verses.

4. Extending the religious applicability of the Bible beyond its originally-intended scope has led to misunderstandings and misapplications of

various verses. One common practice in extending the Bible too easily to ourselves is claiming promises God made to specific people as our own, even if we are not in the same situation as those people and even if the text limits the promise to others. The title of a popular Christian song says about the Bible, "Every Promise in the Book Is Mine." Many Christians are eager to believe that, even though it can be doubted that every promise the Bible made applies to all believers. The *Prayer of Jabez* book and its huge following in the early 2000s is an example of a specific Bible promise of prosperity made to apply to all Christians.[1] Another way to extend the Bible is the "name it and claim it" practice—if we name a promised blessing and claim it as our own, God can be expected to give it to us.

5. Another aspect of extending the relevance of the Bible is making it speak directly and with divine authority on all sorts of topics: dieting and physical health, personal finances, business practices, sports, for instance. Books and articles on these topics abound in the popular Christian press, with titles such as *Financial Peace of Mind from the Word*, *Business by the Bible*, and *The Bible Diet*. However, the Bible has a different view of the scope of its inspiration and authority. When 2 Timothy 3:16–17 states, "All scripture is inspired by God," it immediately states why God inspired it: it is "profitable for teaching, for reproof, for correction, and for training in righteousness, that the [person] of God may be complete, equipped for every good work" (RSV). In other words, Scripture is inspired so that it will be effective for Christian doctrine and life; that should be enough for us. Making the Bible speak directly and systematically about other topics it only touches on will certainly lead to distortions and misuse. (Some evangelical Protestants believe that Scripture does speak with authoritative truth on every topic it speaks about, but many of them also recognize that problems can arise when the Bible is mined for details on topics about which it speaks only occasionally.)

6. "Repurposing" Bible verses, putting them to a different uses than they have in the Bible, usually results in their misuse. People who do this suppose that such a practice is acceptable if it strengthens their faith. For example, Paul's confidence that God will enable him to endure all the trials of his missionary work, "I can do all things through him

---

1. Wilkinson, *The Prayer of Jabez*, 18–75.

who strengthens me" (Philippians 4:13), is often repurposed to bolster our confidence that Christians can reach all the varied goals we set for ourselves. Another example came in a recent radio sermon on Hosea 4:6, "My people are destroyed for a lack of knowledge." This verse refers to the deadly spiritual ignorance of people who worship other gods along with the God of Israel, but the preacher didn't talk about that. Instead, he claimed that a lack of knowledge of the contents of food today is leading to our being physically destroyed. Now, it's certainly a good thing to eat healthy food, but this is not what Hosea had in mind at all. The evangelical biblical scholar Richard Schultz calls such repurposing "textjacking," on analogy with "carjacking."[2] After a while, people even think of the repurposed, textjacked use as the real sense of the verse. Just as carjacking is dangerous to its victims, so textjacking can cause spiritual harm.

7. Religious differences between Christians can produce misunderstandings. Christians today differ strongly on church structure, the sacraments, the work of the Holy Spirit, events at the end of this age, and other matters. Verses on these topics are prone to be misconstrued. For example, Paul's talk about being "caught up in the clouds" in 1 Thessalonians 4:17 is difficult to interpret when Christians disagree over how the Bible speaks about the return of Christ.

8. Political differences between Christians interfere with good Bible interpretation. Politically liberal and conservative Christians can quote the Bible for political purposes. "You shall not kill" (Exodus 20:13), "an eye for an eye" (Exodus 21:24), and "the least of these" (Matthew 25:45), among other biblical phrases, are often used politically. At times people use these verses responsibly, but when reading is influenced by a prior political commitment, a misunderstanding or misapplication will likely result. The Bible has implications for current politics, of course, but most pastors and Bible scholars would probably agree that it has no developed teaching that can be directly applied to modern politics. To quote single verses or parts of verses and apply them to today's politics is often irresponsible.

9. Social and economic differences between Christians can produce misunderstandings. Understanding the Bible can be influenced by one's social class, so the poor, the rich and the middle class can take different

---

2. Schultz, *Out of Context*, 127–28.

approaches to certain passages. Sayings like "The poor you have with you always" (Mark 14:7) can mean something different to rich readers and poor readers. The "prosperity gospel" supposedly anchored in verses such as "Then you will make your way prosperous, and then you will be successful" (Joshua 1:8) has a special appeal to the lower social classes in many areas of the world. Racial and ethnic differences are often connected with these social and economic differences.

10. Cultural differences between the biblical world and the modern West are large and important. If they are not recognized, the differences in cultural context can lead to misunderstandings. People in North America read the Bible with their modern, Western cultural assumptions. For example, American culture emphasizes the individual, but the biblical world tended to be group-oriented. The word *you* in the Bible is usually assumed today to be a singular, but in the Bible it is more often a plural. This can lead to interpretive mistakes—for example when we claim a personal promise when it's really a promise to a whole group. Cultural attitudes to wealth also differ. We think today that desiring to move up the ladder to financial wealth is a good thing, or at least morally neutral, but in biblical culture desiring to move up is morally problematic. This is a significant factor in "The love of money is the root of all evil" (1 Timothy 6:10).

11. Using Bible verses for commercial purposes can distort them. Selling Bible verses on jewelry, clothing, plaques, and other items is big business in the United States. Here are two examples of distorting the Bible by commercializing it. First, an advertisement said in connection with Mark 8:34, "Take Jesus' command to 'carry your cross' literally with [our company's] huge selection of stylish Christian cross rings, Christian wedding rings with crosses, and cross jewelry." Jesus certainly does not mean for us to wear jewelry when he commands his disciples to "carry the cross." Second, several companies use "go the extra mile," an adaptation of Jesus' command in Matthew 5:41, to claim that they make an extra effort in customer service. This phrase in reality speaks about doing good to one's enemies, not about love for one's customers.

12. Using older, outdated versions of the Bible will at times lead to misunderstandings. The English language changes constantly, so using only a translation that is more than one hundred or even fifty years old is

not a good idea. As a case in point, the newer translation, "I treasure your word in my heart" (Psalm 119:11, NRSV), comes much closer to the original Hebrew meaning of this passage than the older "Thy word have I *hid* in my heart" (KJV, RSV). That the King James Version of 1611 is still by far the most used translation in private Bible reading in North America—around 55 percent of Christians who read the Bible privately use the KJV, with 19 percent using the NIV, the second most popular version[3]—means that its readers must sometimes work to avoid the disadvantages of its datedness.

13. Private Bible reading practices can be superficial and reinforce misunderstandings. Private devotional reading of the Bible is an excellent Christian practice and spiritual discipline, to be commended and encouraged. Probably every pastor would like to see church members read the Bible more. But private devotional Bible reading must be done with care. For example, those who read the Bible privately should not only try to discern what God is saying to *me*, but also attend to what God is saying to all Christians today.

14. Small group Bible study can be subjective, and reinforces common misunderstandings. For instance, some small group studies routinely go around the circle asking, "What does this verse mean to you?" The leader then summarizes different responses, compares them to each other, or shapes them into a consensus. This type of Bible study can be inspiring for its participants. However, what is true about private Bible study is also true of group study: it must discern the meaning of the Bible passages in their context and apply this meaning carefully to us today. Happily, group-study leaders can learn how to do this, and there are many good Bible-study guides that help groups to work well with the passages they are studying.

QUESTIONS PEOPLE HAVE ABOUT MISUNDERSTOOD VERSES

When some people hear that their understanding of a Bible verse may be incorrect, they often respond with a question. This is as it should be. Questioning is usually necessary to achieve clarity when we are rethinking our long-held opinions, and sometimes these questions can be sharp. Here are

---

3. Murray, "10 Reasons."

some questions I have heard about misunderstood verses of Scripture, and about efforts to correct these misunderstandings; I offer a brief reply to each.

"If I feel blessed by what might be a misunderstanding, isn't that okay?" Feeling a blessing when we read the Bible can be a good thing. Most misunderstanding of Bible verses is born of a well-intentioned effort to bring to us more of God's blessing, inspiration, and direction. Those who misunderstand verses often get some things right about them, things that can lead to blessing. However, our understanding and use of Bible passages should not be based mainly on our feelings, even a feeling of blessing. Feel-good emotions can be misleading, especially if they are founded on what is mainly a misunderstanding or misuse of Bible verses. Some passages that give us a good feeling should at times actually make us uncomfortable.

"Is it wrong if a verse is misunderstood or misused to make an otherwise true biblical point?" The short answer is yes. We should not be so casual with Scripture that we impose a new meaning on a biblical verse, even if this meaning can find support in the wider Bible. Some people are careful to admit, "I know that this isn't the main point of this passage," and then go on to make a point that doesn't come at all from the passage, but from another part of the Bible. If the point we are making has biblical support, we should make it from an appropriate text. "Sound teaching from the wrong text" is a practice that sooner or later will lead to problems.

"Haven't people been misinterpreting verses for a long time?" Yes, there have been misunderstandings of the Bible for a very long time—in fact, for as long as people have been reading the Bible. Even within the New Testament itself we find a warning about how some Christians are misunderstanding the letters of Paul (2 Peter 3:15–16). The biblical scholar Henry Wansbrough could title his book on the history of Bible interpretation *The Use and Abuse of the Bible*, because good interpretation and misinterpretation have existed together from the first centuries of Christianity until now.[4] However, the problem of misunderstanding the Bible may be more serious today, according to some who have been watching this trend. Books from some popular Christian authors, commercial uses of Bible verses on posters and plaques, and especially discussion of verses on the Internet have all contributed to the recent growth and popularity of misunderstandings.

---

4. Wansbrough, *Use and Abuse of the Bible*.

"Doesn't the popularity of such interpretations among Christians show that God is using them?" Many misunderstood verses explained in this book are indeed very popular. However, popularity itself does not guarantee truth, and misunderstanding God's Word does not glorify God. Of course, God can use our mistakes for good, but that is no reason for us to be careless in reading the Bible. A theologian once wrote, "Evil remains evil, in spite of the good which God may bring out of it."[5] Similarly, bad interpretation remains bad, despite God's bringing good things out of it.

"How can I avoid misunderstanding Bible verses when I'm not a Bible scholar?" For almost all the verses we deal with in this book, it doesn't take an expert to figure out the correct meaning. The Bible was not written for scholars, and one need not be a scholar to grasp its basic meaning. Some parts of the Bible are admittedly more difficult to interpret, and laypeople may want to consult an expert commentary. However, when ordinary Christians read the Bible carefully, using their intellectual and spiritual skills, and informed by good reading practices, they can avoid most common misunderstandings.

HOW CAN WE READ THE BIBLE BETTER?

As I said above, the basic meaning of the Bible can usually be discerned by ordinary Christian readers. Many Christians, however, want to advance in their understanding of the Bible. What can they do to understand their favorite verses, and indeed the whole Bible, more carefully? All Christians who read the Bible, not just church leaders, should aspire to handle it correctly. I offer these as suggested guidelines for more careful Bible reading, especially to avoid misunderstandings.

1. Don't read or ponder only one verse—ever! The writers of the Bible did not use verse numbers, which were added in the 1500s. The Geneva Bible (1560) and the King James Bible (1611) indented every verse, making each look like a paragraph. Many printings of the King James Version still do this. This practice may imply that each verse is an independent, developed thought, which it is not. Most versions of the Bible published today don't do this any longer, but the implication that each verse has a meaning unto itself still lingers in the mind of many Christians. As a result, reading single verses today is unwise.

---

5. Barth, *Epistle to the Romans*, 84.

Instead, read and ponder verses in their whole-passage context. For example, if you know John 3:16 by memory, as many do, understanding the verses before it will make it mean even more, and you will know fully what "[God] gave his only Son" means.

2. Recognize the differences between genres (types of writing) in the Bible when you read, because interpretation is significantly influenced by what genre we think we are encountering. We do recognize different genres almost instinctively when reading other material such as newspapers or websites, and we should learn to do this with the Bible as well. The first thing to realize is that "the Bible" is not a genre, but a whole collection of them. For example, biblical proverbs differ from commandments, although proverbs often have clear moral implications. Also, biblical poetry with its more elusive, emotional language differs from prose. For example, those who interpret "borne up on eagles' wings" literally—that the people of Israel were all carried to safety by a big bird, which someone actually said about Psalm 91—will miss the point made there. This is a silly example, of course, but silly and sad examples abound of what happens when genre is ignored.

3. After reflecting carefully on a passage and sticking with it for a while, consider its place in the whole Bible. What might your favorite verse mean for the whole biblical book in which it is found? What might it mean in the big sweep of Scripture? This may stretch your knowledge of the Bible, and call for you to learn more about it. A good study Bible with cross-references and explanatory notes will help with this. The more we can use Scripture to interpret Scripture, the fuller and more accurate our reading of the Bible will be.

4. Read beforehand the Scripture passages used in your church services, if you can. Many churches publish in advance their Sunday Scripture readings. If you read these before the service, and compare your understanding with what is said about the text in the sermon, you can train yourself in understanding the Bible better. You can also develop your skills in relating the Bible to contemporary life. Experiencing the Bible as the Word of God is meant to be done among the people of God, and we should let worship shape our experience of the Word and our ability to understand it and live in it.

5. Reflect on the challenge in your favorite verses, not just the comfort and promise they bring you. This should be done in both private

reading and group study. The Bible was not written only to comfort and encourage the people of God. It was also written to challenge and correct them. Reading to discern the Bible's corrective for our lives will be beneficial in the long run, even if it feels uncomfortable or even painful at the time.

6. If you have a need to go deeper, find a commentary you trust. Several respected Bible scholars have published commentaries suitable for use by laypeople. Perhaps the best series is by N. T. Wright, The New Testament for Everyone, which has a concise treatment for every book in the New Testament.[6] Its valuable companion series is by John Goldingay, The Old Testament for Everyone.[7] One-volume Bible commentaries don't go into a lot of interpretive details, so they can often be used profitably by lay readers.[8] Here is a word of warning, however: Use free commentaries posted on websites with caution. Although they may be "classic" commentaries, they are usually more than seventy-five years old and are based on even older translations of the Bible. They typically have limited value in helping today's readers make good applications from the text to contemporary issues.

Now let's begin our study of twenty-four misunderstood verses.

---

6. Wright, New Testament for Everyone, in 18 volumes.
7. Goldingay, Old Testament for Everyone, in 17 volumes.
8 For example, see Dunn and Rogerson, eds., *Eerdmans Commentary on the Bible*.

1

What Is the Mark of Cain?

The Lord put a mark on Cain, so that no one who came upon him would kill him. (Genesis 4:15)

"The mark of Cain" has long been misunderstood as a part of God's punishment of Cain for killing his brother Abel. Cain received this mark, and it has continued, or so people think, on other people through time until today. In the Middle Ages, Christians called the badges that Jews were forced to wear in public the "mark of Cain." Nazi leaders serving prison sentences after World War II sometimes complained to prison chaplains that they bore the "mark of Cain." Some convicts in Russian prisons today have called the tattoos that they give to each other in prison the "mark of Cain."

One particular idea about the mark of Cain held that it is black skin. This seems obviously racist today, but until quite recently it was a widespread notion. From the 1600s well into the 1900s, many Americans and Europeans thought that Cain's "mark" was black skin and that all black people are Cain's spiritual descendants and still under a divine curse. For example, the tenth president of the Latter-day Saint church, Joseph Fielding Smith Jr., wrote in 1931, "It was well understood by the early elders of the [Mormon] Church that the mark which was placed on Cain and which his posterity inherited was black skin."[1] This belief was used by the LDS

---

1. Smith, *Way to Perfection*, 107.

Church to deny their priesthood to African and African American men, a policy that lasted until 1978. Mormons were not alone in this faulty interpretation of the mark of Cain. It served as one of several rationalizations among Protestant and Catholic Christians for the enslavement of millions of Africans from the 1500s to the 1800s, and it continued into the 1900s as a factor in racial discrimination against African Americans.

The racist interpretation of "the mark of Cain" has largely disappeared in the last fifty years or so, but the expression "the mark of Cain" is still common. Today the "mark of Cain" is understood in a variety of dictionaries as a "curse," a "sign of guilt," a "stigma of shame," and even "a person's sinful nature." Apart from the expression, negative connotations persist in our culture around the single word "Cain." For example, "raising Cain" is a common expression today for bad behavior, especially by children and teenagers. A 2000 book about troubled boys in the United States was titled *Raising Cain*,[2] as was a 2005 PBS-TV documentary based on it.

When we look at Genesis 4:15 in its context, the correct meaning of "the mark of Cain" becomes clear. Cain was the first child of Adam and Eve, born after their expulsion from the garden of Eden, and his brother Abel followed. Cain became a farmer, Abel a herder (Genesis 4:1–2), the two main occupations of Old Testament times. When God accepted Abel's animal offering but rejected Cain's offering of fruits, Cain was angry, and his anger festered (vv. 3–5). Despite God's command to Cain to deal with his sin before it overwhelmed him (vv. 6–7), that sin in fact did overwhelm him. Cain murdered his brother (v. 8), the first death to occur in the world. He lied to God when God confronted him about Abel's whereabouts: "I do not know," and then added the words that have become infamous as a guilty evasion: "Am I my brother's keeper?" (v. 9). God punished Cain by making his efforts at farming a complete failure, and Cain realized that this would make him "a fugitive and a wanderer on the earth" (vv. 11–12). Adam and Eve had been exiled from the garden, but now Cain would be exiled even farther. When Cain complained that "anyone who meets me may kill me," God replied: "Therefore whoever kills Cain, vengeance will be taken on him sevenfold" (vv. 13–15). Then comes the misunderstood verse: "The LORD put a mark on Cain, so that no one who came upon him would kill him." In a short time, Cain went from God to Nod: "Then Cain went out from the presence of the LORD, and settled in the land of Nod, east of Eden (v. 16). Cain and his wife had a child (v. 17). (This verse has prompted many

---

2. Kindlon and Thompson, *Raising Cain*.

a skeptic to ask, where did Cain's wife come from?) The rest of Genesis 4 narrates briefly the contributions of Cain's descendants to the beginnings of human civilization, as herders, musicians, and metalworkers.

When set in this context, it's obvious what the "mark of Cain" means. It was not a punishment or a curse; it was a protection. Jewish interpreters have almost to a person seen this correctly, but Christians have not. Cain's real punishment was divine rejection from the ground. God had punished Adam by making his farming difficult (Genesis 3:17–19), and now God punished Cain by making his farming impossible. This forced him to become a wanderer. The mark God put on him was to keep him alive, and to judge from the whole narrative of Genesis 4, it was effective in doing this.

Why did Cain need this protection? Likely because he was a murderer, and even at the beginning of human life (as today), murder was among the most serious of crimes and had to be punished. Cain worried aloud to God that he was especially vulnerable to a deadly attack that would avenge his killing of Abel. God's protective mark on him was effective, and Cain lived a long life. He had descendants who made a significant contribution to the spread of human life in the world, even though they were prone to the violence that he brought to the world (4:17–24). The rest of the Bible sees Cain as a murderer and liar (1 John 3:12) and an example of someone who follows a godless way of life (Jude 1:11). Jewish writings from the first centuries BCE share these viewpoints, particularly Wisdom of Solomon 10:3: "But when the unrighteous man [Cain] went away from her [Wisdom] in his anger, he perished also in the fury with which he murdered his brother." In 4 Maccabees 18:11 Cain is first in a line of those who persecute the righteous. In Jubilees 4:5 Cain is cursed to wander. None of these treatments of Cain outside of Genesis mentions Cain's mark.

The practice of marking people for their protection can be found in other places in the Bible. God commanded that a mark be put on the foreheads of the people in Jerusalem who were repentant: "Go through the city, through Jerusalem, and put a mark on the foreheads of those who sigh and groan over all the abominations that are committed in it" (Ezekiel 9:4). This mark will protect them from the coming destruction of the city. The book of Revelation features three episodes where people have a mark placed upon them. A special group of people, the 144,000 believers, receives a mark from God on their foreheads that guarantees their protection (Revelation 7:3). The mark in Ezekiel and the mark in Revelation 7 keep God's people safe from impending judgment. In the book of Revelation we also find a sinister mark, the "mark of the beast." The beast will mark all those who worship him with his name and number on their right hand or on their forehead (Revelation 13:16; see also 14:9, 11; 16:2; 19:20). The final example of marking in the Bible, the only mark to endure for eternity, is a happy one. At the final consummation of all things, all the redeemed will be marked with the name of Jesus Christ: "They will see his face, and his name will be on their foreheads" (Revelation 22:4). This mark shows that they belong to Jesus.

Seen in the context of its passage in Genesis 4 and the wider biblical testimony about marking, the "mark of Cain" is clearly a protection. This mark, whatever it was, was not a curse on Cain but a rescue from the effects of his curse. Its purpose is to keep Cain from being killed by others. To judge from other biblical passages that feature marking, it was in all likelihood a mark on Cain's body, not his clothing. It would have to be visible to others, such as on his forehead or one of his hands. Genesis gives no hint about what the mark looked like. It may have looked threatening in order to ward off harm, perhaps threatening the "sevenfold vengeance" that God promised to those who might kill Cain. However, some protective marks in the ancient Near East, such as the all-seeing eye of the Egyptian god Horus, did not look threatening. It may have been a mark that people saw as representing God or God's name, as in Revelation 22:4. Obviously, we can't be sure what the mark was. We can be certain of one thing: the mark serves a positive purpose, to keep Cain alive—the first killer is not killed—so that he can contribute despite his flaws to the growth and spread of humankind. Somehow this mark communicated to others that Cain was not to be harmed. If it was like other markings in the Bible discussed above, it may have shown that Cain belonged to God. Whatever the mark was, this positive purpose of the mark is so obvious in the text that one wonders how thinking about the mark itself as a punishment ever arose!

What might this misinterpretation of Genesis 4:15 get right? Very little, it's sad to say. It does correctly recognize that Cain's mark is put on him by God, but it confuses Cain's punishment with his protection. It also fails to recognize that the "mark of Cain" was a one-time thing. There is no hint in Genesis that it continues among Cain's descendants, or that anyone else today can get the "mark of Cain."

What is the meaning of this verse in its context for us today? To see this, we will have to look beyond Cain as a murderer, and see in Genesis 4 how God handles this murderer. The first point for Christians today is this:

Sin can "crouch at the door" waiting to pounce on us as well, as it did for Cain. Sin's "desire is for you," God warns Cain, "but you must master it" (v. 7). If we become sullen and frustrated over how we think God is treating us, as Cain did, the pounce may be especially close. Evil may not crouch and pounce on us as dramatically as it did with Cain, but it crouches nonetheless. The warning that God gave to Cain is typical of God's warning to all his children who struggle with sin: Sin is looking to attack, and we must deal with it.

Here is a second, more positive point from the corrected understanding of this passage for Christians today. When God deals with sin in this life, either directly or indirectly, a part of God's purpose is often protection of the sinner. This protection graciously gives "time for amendment of life," an eloquent phrase from the prayer book of the Church of England. By the standards of justice in the Old Testament, Cain deserved to die for his crime of murder. God did punish Cain severely, so much that he complained, "My punishment is more than I can bear!" But God mercifully preserved his life so that Cain could make some contribution to human society. Of course, we shouldn't presume on God's mercy by thinking that God will always preserve us from serious consequences if we commit serious sins. That is not the correct conclusion to draw from the Cain story! Instead, we should look on any mercy God may show us as a part of God's discipline for his people. God doesn't automatically write off sinners, and maybe we shouldn't either.

QUESTIONS FOR REFLECTION AND DISCUSSION

1. Before you began this section, what did you think that the mark of Cain was?
2. What is the significance of death entering the world by way of a brother murdering a brother?
3. How does the misunderstanding of Genesis 4:15 take this verse out of context?
4. How might you explain why, when the mark of Cain is so explicitly a protection in Genesis 4, it soon came to be understood by Christians from ancient times through today as a punishment?

5. What have been some of the consequences of perpetuating the idea that the mark of Cain is punishment and means being black? How is this is a sobering example of the danger of misinterpreting Scripture?

6. The image of "sin crouching at the door" like a predatory animal is a vivid one. Have you experienced temptation or sin in this way?

2

Is "Mizpah" a Benediction?

Therefore the name of it was called ... Mizpah; for Laban said, "The Lord watch between me and thee, when we are absent one from another." (Genesis 31:48–49)

IN MY SUNDAY SCHOOL when I was a boy, all the students and teachers met together before we went off to our classes. At the end of this session the teacher in charge said, "Let's stand and say the Mizpah Benediction." We all rose and dutifully recited the end of Genesis 31:49 from the King James Version (given above), thinking that it was a happy blessing: "The Lord watch between me and thee, when we are absent one from another."

    The so-called Mizpah Benediction is widely used today by Christians as they part from each other. They sometimes recite it at the conclusion of church meetings. Ministers will use it as a benediction to close services of worship. It has worked its way onto greeting cards, wall plaques, refrigerator magnets, wedding rings, and even headstones in cemeteries. A line of Mizpah jewelry charms still popular today goes all the way back to the 1850s in England. Mizpah jewelry is given as an expression of friendship or love between two people, either with "May the Lord watch between you and me" or only the word "Mizpah" on it. The popular Mizpah pendant is usually broken into two pieces, with the words of Genesis 31:49 also broken between the pieces. When the friends, the engaged couple, or the spouses are reunited, the two pieces are put together, and the full Mizpah benediction appears. In sum, the "Mizpah Benediction" is a popular verse, and most people today look on it as a beautiful blessing. But as we will see, this is a significant misunderstanding.

How does this verse appear in Genesis? As you might remember, Jacob was often in conflict with his family, usually conflict of his own making. He and his twin brother, Esau, were locked in competition with each other literally from birth. After swindling Esau and deceiving his father to obtain the larger share of the family inheritance, Jacob has to leave his home in a hurry. He goes to a faraway land to live with his uncle Laban. As Genesis 31 opens, Jacob has been working for Laban for twenty years. They distrust each other deeply, in a way that only two scoundrels can. Each claims that the other has cheated him. Jacob still resents that Laban switched his older daughter, Leah, for his more beautiful younger daughter, Rachel, in their marriage ceremony and then demanded seven years' more work for Rachel. Laban knows that Jacob had manipulated the breeding of Laban's sheep to give himself the best flocks. Then Jacob flees in secret with Laban's daughters and grandchildren "like captives of the sword" (v. 26), and with the flocks and herds that Laban considers his. Laban and his armed men pursue and overtake Jacob's group, and tense accusations fly between them.

In this dangerous situation, Laban proposes that they reach a new, sacred agreement to deal with their disputes. He suggests that they "agree to disagree," as we say today: they should go their separate ways and stay away from each other. This would prevent them from harming each other directly. They set up a pillar stone as a sign of this agreement, and they both pile up other stones around this pillar. Then Laban says,

> 48 "This heap of stones is a witness between you and me today." Therefore he called it "Galeed" ["heap of witness"], 49 and the pillar "Mizpah" ["watchtower"], for he said, "The LORD watch between you and me, when we are absent one from the other. 50 If you ill-treat my daughters, or if you take wives in addition to my daughters, though no one is with us, remember that God is witness between you and me. . . . 52 This heap is a witness, and the pillar is a witness, that I will not pass beyond this heap to you, and you will not pass beyond this heap and this pillar to me, for harm."
> (Genesis 31:48–50, 52)

Various ceremonies are then carried out to seal the agreement before God. This agreement proposed by Laban is all the more impressive in that Laban served different gods from the God of Jacob. The chapter ends with a touching scene, as Laban kisses his daughters and his grandchildren and blesses them before they depart with Jacob.

The stones that mark this agreement need a bit of explanation. The ancient Israelites often set up a single large stone to commemorate an event. They put no inscription on it; people would have to remember why the stone was there. This passage also says that a mound ("heap") of stones was piled up around this single stone, also for the sake of remembrance. So many stones were piled up that Laban compares them to a watchtower. Watchtowers were often found in vineyards. They were constructed of stone, and some doubled as olive presses or wine presses. Although the pile of stones Laban saw did not form an actual watchtower, Laban called it that. *Mizpah* means generally a "lookout point," and more specifically a "watchtower." After these stones are put in place and their meaning is agreed to when Jacob and Laban name them, there are sacrifices and a common meal.

Now we come to the heart of the misunderstanding. In this story, "watch between" clearly does not mean "watch over" or "keep safe," as the common misunderstanding of this verse assumes. It's not a happy or positive saying, and it doesn't mean "God be with you till we meet again." Instead, "watch between us" means "guard us from each other." It can be paraphrased, "May God watch you while I can't." This is confirmed by what follows: "even if no one is with us, God is a witness between us." Their agreement calls on God to monitor Jacob's and Laban's observance of the covenant they have made, and it implies that God will punish the one who doesn't observe the agreement. The key word, "watchtower," bears out this "God-watches-you-while-I-can't" meaning, because a watchtower is used to watch for approaching enemies, not for returning friends. Jacob and Laban had a close relationship in family and business, but they certainly were not friends.

Clearly, a large gap has grown between the original meaning of this verse and the way it is misunderstood today. How did this big misunderstanding arise? We can't be certain, but as I said above, it goes back to the mid-1800s in England. This was a time when many couples were separated as the man went off alone for government service or commerce in the far-flung British Empire. Mizpah jewelry reached its height of popularity during World War I among couples separated by the war. When this verse is misconstrued, it is a happy mutual blessing of two people who are parting, signifying a strong emotional bond between them. Even though its actual meaning in Genesis does not fit the use Christians make of it today, when taken out of its context this verse is indeed meaningful and comforting. So it was pressed into service for this purpose.

What might this misunderstanding get right about this passage? It does correctly understand that God watches us at all times, as Christians who emphasize this verse believe. This is indeed a blessing. Observers of the modern church scene in North America say that many Christians' sense of the presence of God in their personal lives is weak—so weak that some Christians sadly have no sense of the presence of God. So it's not unexpected that the Mizpah saying in Genesis would become, against its meaning in context, a reminder of God's presence when we are absent from loved ones, especially loved ones who remind us of God's presence. We can take comfort in the assurance that God is present in such times, although this particular verse doesn't offer this comfort and should not be used to do so.

The corrected understanding of this verse means three things for Christian life today. First, God still watches *between* people, not only *over* them. In other words, God is present with us not only to protect us but also to correct us. God does watch over friends, but this verse says that God watches between people who don't get along, at times to protect them from each other. God cares about the quality of our relationships in our homes, churches, business and neighborhoods. When we do wrong to each other, God knows about it and can act through God's people to correct it. An example of this from the New Testament is the apostle Paul's rebuke of Euodia and Syntyche; he urges them on God's behalf to settle their problems, and appoints a mediator between them (Philippians 4:2–3). The Mizpah saying reminds us that God watches between us to encourage us to do what is right. It urges us to keep our agreements, and to keep the peace between God's people.

A second meaning for today comes from the context of this passage. Negotiation and practical compromise, which happen as Laban and Jacob reach and carry out the Mizpah agreement, are possible solutions to family troubles. Continued conflicts lead to further breakdown of family relationships. The same is true in our churches. Compromise does not make anyone completely happy, but it's too much to suppose that Christians can always settle their differences completely and to everyone's satisfaction. Partial reconciliation is better than no reconciliation at all.

A final meaning is this: compromise can lead to a brighter future. In a tense situation, Jacob and Laban agree to deal with their troubles with the Mizpah agreement. They are not really reconciled to each other, but they "agree to disagree" and not pass the Mizpah marker to do harm to each other. For the rest of Genesis, this is carried out. This arrangement works, and there is no more trouble between Jacob and Laban. Even today, knowing that God is watching between us can help Christians to do what is right. In sum, "Mizpah" is not a blessing, but acting on the knowledge that God is watching between us can indeed bring a blessing.

QUESTIONS FOR REFLECTION AND DISCUSSION

1. Why might Laban have been the one to propose the Mizpah solution to the conflict with Jacob?

2. Do you think that misunderstanding this verse as "May God watch over us and keep us safe" offers us a different view of God than does "May God watch between us and keep us safe from each other"? How so?

3. A modern proverb says, "Good fences make good neighbors." What might the careful reading of the Mizpah story suggest in regard to that proverb? How does this fit with the testimony of the entire Bible? What does it imply for us in our everyday lives as Christ followers?

4. Do an Internet search for the term "Mizpah jewelry," and examine this merchandise. What are your impressions of how this jewelry uses this verse?

5. What might be lost if we misunderstand this particular verse?

6. What can we glean from this passage in regard to tolerance and reconciliation? To what relationship or situation in your own life or in your church might this passage apply so that you can move forward?

3

What Killing Does God Forbid?

You shall not kill. (Exodus 20:13)

LIKE SOME OF THE Ten Commandments, this commandment is very brief, only two words in Hebrew. The brevity of these commandments is both a strength and a weakness. Later passages in Israelite, Jewish and Christian tradition explain most of these commandments and fill out their meaning so that they could be effective in daily life. Although this was done for "You shall not kill," many people still wonder, To what does "You shall not kill" apply today? (Some Christians, perhaps you, find thinking about killing difficult, but it's an important topic today, and positive things come out of this commandment.) Biblical scholars agree that the range of "kill" is a key interpretive issue in this commandment,[1] and this is true for laypeople as well. "You shall not kill" means at the least that God forbids taking of life. But exactly what kind of killing does God forbid? After all, "kill" is a broad word, and the positive "reverence for life" idea that grows out of this commandment can apply to many things. Those who argue for a wider meaning of "You shall not kill" say that this commandment forbids the following:

- Killing animals. A growing religiously based animal rights movement sometimes applies "You shall not kill" to animals. All life is to be respected, they say, not just human life. Animals should not be killed for sport, for food, or for any other reason. This feeling for animals is not

1. Stamm and Andrew, *Ten Commandments in Recent Research*, 98–99.

confined to special-interest activists or to controversial scholars such as Peter Singer of Princeton University, who argues that an individual human life is no more intrinsically valuable than the life of an individual animal.[2] Many ordinary people have a deep respect for animal life (if not as radically as Singer has), a respect rooted for many in this commandment. For example, in a television news report on a recent West Michigan killing, the neighbor of the victim said to a reporter, "The guy murdered my neighbor, and then he murdered his dog," as if these were equal acts. He was speaking in grief, of course, but his words are telling.

- Killing in war. Christian pacifists have consistently claimed that this commandment applies to warfare, so Christians may not serve in the military. They consider all killing in war to be wrong, not only killing done contrary to international law and the rules of war. Pacifist elements were strong in the ancient church, reappeared in parts of the Reformation, and in modern times spread from parts of the church like the Quakers to the wider society. Preston Sprinkle points to ancient church history after the New Testament and concludes, "While early Christian writers were divided on many issues . . . , when it came to killing their voices seemed to be unanimous: Believers are prohibited from taking human life."[3]

- Capital punishment. When the death penalty is carried out in the United States, protesters regularly gather outside the prison walls to demonstrate against capital punishment. One or more of them typically carries a sign that says, "You shall not kill." The practice of the government killing people because they killed others seems particularly wrong to them, and lacking in common sense. Why do so many American Christians believe that the Bible opposes the death penalty? The answer given most often is that the King James Version read by American Protestants and the versions of the Bible read by most Roman Catholics give Exodus 20:13 and Deuteronomy 5:17 as, "Thou shalt not kill," not "Thou shalt not murder." This opens the door for many to apply "You shall not kill" to capital punishment itself.

- Abortion. Abortion remains one of the most charged moral issues in the United States today. Opposition to abortion most often comes

---

2. Singer, *Animal Liberation*.
3. Sprinkle, *Fight*, 200.

from a religious perspective, and typically cites this commandment. For example, the official *Catechism of the Catholic Church* deals with abortion in the section on "You shall not kill."[4] This verse's support for the value of individual human lives is a foundation of the pro-life position. "You shall not kill human life in the womb" is an obvious meaning of this commandment for millions of Christians today, both Roman Catholics and Protestants.

What is the correct meaning of this commandment? To put it in more detail, is this commandment, in its biblical context, speaking about killing animals, or killing in war, capital punishment, or abortion? In a word, no. This verse is widely misunderstood mainly because it is applied to things that it was not intended to cover. Of course these four contemporary issues are important for the church today, and many other passages in the Bible speak about them, directly or indirectly. The key issue here is this: Can *this verse* from the Ten Commandments be correctly used to support these positions? Here are reasons for thinking that it cannot.

First, on killing animals: the Old Testament and the New Testament do not apply this commandment to killing other living things. Only humans are made in the image of God. This image-of-God idea is important in the command not to murder (Genesis 9:6). In some South Asian religions, "Do not kill" or "Do no harm" does mean not killing animals, and this leads to a vegetarian diet, even to walking very carefully to avoid stepping on insects. The Bible knows none of this. In the Bible killing a neighbor's animal is a crime, but it's a property crime not equivalent to killing a human being. Few people today would defend the wanton killing of animals; it's cruel and senseless, and in many societies it is illegal. But this commandment does not speak about this.

Second, on killing in war: this is tolerated, even at times commanded in the Old Testament. But the Old Testament also lays down rules for warfare, such as who may participate and how war is to be conducted. The New Testament is largely silent on the participation of Christians in warfare, although some interpreters conclude that Romans 13 leans toward it. This is why Preston Sprinkle's argument against Christian participation in warfare must be drawn from post–New Testament writings.

As for capital punishment, it's hard to argue that capital punishment is a violation of the biblical meaning of "You shall not murder" when the

---

4. Catholic Church, "Respect for Human Life," in *The Catechism of the Catholic Church*, part 3, section 2, chapter 2, article 5, section 1.

book of Exodus, indeed wherever the Old Testament deals with this topic, commands that murderers be put to death. The death penalty is commanded precisely because the image of God was in the person who had been murdered. This reasoning might seem contradictory to us today, but it fits the biblical context, and that's what we must reckon with at some point in Christian moral reflection. Jesus saved the life of a woman about to be put to death for adultery (John 7:53—8:11) but passed no judgment on the death penalty itself. The so-called good thief on the cross says that he and other thief are getting their just punishment, words that the gospel author implicitly approves (Luke 23:39-43). The apostle Paul talks about the "sword" and the right of the state to take the lives of evildoers (Romans 13:4). Even if we don't put murderers to death in many states and Canadian provinces, largely out of opposition to the death penalty, in a sense we still deprive murderers of life if we confine them to prison for the rest of their lives.

Finally, on abortion: the practice of abortion is unknown in the Old Testament, and in all likelihood would have been rejected if it had been known. Still, the punishment for accidental killing of a child in the womb (Exodus 21:22) is an indication that children in the womb were not considered on par with children after birth. The morality of abortion can—and should—be judged by biblical and theological factors, especially the respect for human life that the Bible demands; but the original, direct meaning of this commandment does not have anything to do with the contemporary abortion debate. In conclusion, the commandment "You shall not kill" has a limited meaning: it prohibits the illegal killing of another human being. Does this more restricted meaning make this verse mean less? Not at all; in fact, it reinforces its power by focusing on the kind of killing that God means to forbid in this commandment.

Now we should take a closer look at this commandment in its context. First, different Bible translations give different wording for this verse. This increases the misunderstanding, but also points the way to a correct understanding. Two different Hebrew words come into play here. One means "put to death, kill," and the other, used in the commandment, means "murder." The King James Version reads "Thou shalt not kill," and since the KJV continues to be influential as the single most used Bible in North America, the misunderstanding of the verse continues. "Murder" in the Ten Commandments means intentional and illegal killing of another human, so it does not cover valid capital punishment or valid killing in warfare. However, it also covers things we might consider less than murder, such as causing death by deliberate carelessness or neglect—in the famous law of the goring ox, for example (Exodus 21:28–32). That is why most recent translations render this commandment "You shall not murder" (see, for example, the New Revised Standard Version, the New International Version, and the New Jewish Publication Society Bible) rather than "You shall not kill."

What does the misunderstanding of this verse—that it applies directly to a wide range of killing—get right? It correctly understands that the law in this verse is foundational. "You shall not murder" provides the basic meaning of God's intent, but it is meant to be expanded. The misunderstanding also correctly understands that the verse talks about life and respect for life. The issue is, how far should it be expanded, and in what direction? We should follow the Bible itself in this. We might want to add other moral perspectives and guidelines beyond the Bible from our own religious traditions, but we ought to speak accurately about what the Bible says and doesn't say.

What is the meaning of this command, rightly understood, for us today? To answer this we must take a wider view of the topic in the Bible. Why do humans murder, and why is it such a grievous act? First, the Bible's command against murder does not rest on a social consensus—baldly put, that killing people is disruptive to society—but on how God created the world. Humans are created in God's image (Genesis 1:27), and we were made to live in harmony with God and other humans. Although God had warned the man and the woman that on the day they ate of the forbidden fruit they would die (Genesis 2:17), the first death actually came when Cain killed his brother Abel (Genesis 4:8). From that day forward, taking the lives of others has been too commonplace, and at times human life is even "cheap," as we say. However, to God every life is important, even precious, because every human bears the divine image. This commandment, "You shall not murder," still connects us with the deep meaning of God's creation of human life in God's image.

Second, we must see the broader the meaning of this commandment to keep its intent. It forbids murdering another person, but the Old Testament shows how this commandment was understood in this broader sense, as laying a foundation for wide respect for human life. For example, we must not punish people accused of killing unless they are tried and convicted (Numbers 35:12). We must not endanger human life (Leviticus 19:16). We must not mock a deaf person or put a stumbling block in the way of a blind person, an act both cruel and dangerous (Leviticus 19:14). We are not to seek revenge or even bear a grudge against someone. Instead, we must "love your neighbor as yourself" (Leviticus 19:18). Martin Luther's *Small Catechism* puts the positive meaning of "You shall not murder" well: "We are so to fear and love God that we do not endanger or harm the lives of our neighbors, but instead help and support them in all of life's needs."[5] Of course the ultimate expression of respect for human life is in Jesus' command to "love your enemies" (Matthew 5:44; Luke 6:27, 35).

Third, Christians should follow carefully Jesus' reinterpretation of this commandment in the Sermon on Mount. Jesus taught his disciples that anger against a "brother or sister," referring to followers of Jesus, and angrily speaking evil against them, will bring one under divine judgment for a murderous emotion. Jesus commands his followers to "be reconciled to your brother or sister" before bringing a sacrifice to God (Matthew 5:21–26). The effect of this reinterpretation of this commandment is to trace murder to its root in the human heart and deal with it there. There will be no acted-out murder if this is done, and respect for human life will increase. This teaching of Jesus, which is intentionally radical and challenging, is echoed in "All who hate a brother or sister are murderers, and you know that murderers do not have eternal life abiding in them" (1 John 3:15). When we harbor hatred in our hearts for another person, we have committed the sin of murder in God's eyes, but when we deal with hatred as Jesus commanded, our lives will become more like God intended them to be.

QUESTIONS FOR REFLECTION AND DISCUSSION

1. How would you explain the relationship of the narrow command "You shall not murder" with the wider biblical command to respect and protect human life?

2. What are the similarities and the differences between having "murder in our hearts" and committing murder in deed?

3. Some Christians can easily think that they have fully kept the "You shall not murder" command because they haven't literally killed anyone. How does an understanding of the wider meaning of this commandment correct that thinking?

---

5. Luther, *Luther's Small Catechism*, 26.

4. What are some practical ways that we can carry out the wider meaning of "You shall not murder" as expressed by Martin Luther?

5. What might this commandment mean for killings of people by the police, so controversial as this book is being written? Or for killings of police officers?

6. How does commandment "You shall not murder" relate to the other nine commandments, especially in the second table of the law (the commands about Sabbath rest through coveting)?

4

Is "An Eye for an Eye" Vengeance?

If any harm follows, then you shall give life for life, eye for eye, tooth for tooth, hand for hand, foot for foot, burn for burn, wound for wound, stripe for stripe. (Exodus 21:23–25)

MOST PEOPLE TODAY UNDERSTAND "an eye for an eye" as a system of vengeance or retaliation. That's the way it is used in popular culture today—as, for example, in the 1996 film *An Eye for an Eye*, in which usually mild-mannered Sally Field plays a character who seeks private, vengeful retribution for the murder of her daughter. Some people use this Bible verse to justify getting revenge, saying that the Bible rightly commands us to take "an eye for an eye." But this is the minority opinion. Most people think any practice of "an eye for an eye" is a bad idea, even barbaric. Mohandas Gandhi, the leader of Indian independence from Great Britain in the 1940s, famously said that "An eye for an eye makes the whole world blind." For numerous Christians, Jesus' warning to his followers against this "eye-for-an-eye" principle in the Sermon on the Mount (Matthew 5:38–42) suggests that it no longer has any value at all—and maybe never did. Many Christians today regard it as another of the Old Testament laws that don't apply to us today.

What does this famous saying in Exodus 21 actually mean? It's a verse that looks clear enough without too much effort, so most people don't think deeply about its meaning. Like all short sayings in the Bible, "an eye for an eye" must be read in its context to determine its correct meaning. In Exodus, it is designed as a step up from uncontrolled violence, especially from bloody feuds that went on for years, even generations. Societies built on the social values of protecting one's honor are especially prone to feuds. The societies of the ancient Near East, including Israelite society, functioned on the principle of gaining honor and, if need be, restoring lost honor. If somebody harms you, they must be harmed in return, or your position in society will diminish. But as we will see, it is a misunderstanding to think that "an eye for an eye" is a prescription for vengeance.

At this point, we should take a closer look at the entire "eye-for-an eye" passage in Exodus 21:22–27:

> 22 When two men who are fighting injure a pregnant woman so that she miscarries, but no further harm comes to her, those responsible shall be fined what the woman's husband demands, paying as much as the judges determine. 23 If any other harm does come to her, then you shall give life for life, 24 eye for eye, tooth for tooth, hand for hand, foot for foot, 25 burn for burn, wound for wound, stripe for stripe. 26 When a master strikes the eye of a male or female slave and destroys it, the owner shall let the slave go as a free person, to compensate for the eye. 27 If the owner knocks out a tooth of a male or female slave, the slave shall be freed to compensate for the tooth.

Notice here that if a slave is the victim in an "eye-for-eye" or "tooth-for-tooth" incident, the slave's injuries lead to freedom for the slave as correct compensation. Correct compensation for a slave's injury does not involve inflicting a retaliatory injury upon the master—knocking out the master's eye or tooth, or levying any other physical punishment. This provision shows clearly that "an eye for an eye" is a principle; it is not to be applied literally.

"An eye for an eye" is a principle of public, official justice in the Bible, but it is *never* a matter of private justice or vengeance—of "payback," we call it. The public nature of this principle prevents private feuds, but it also prevents the government, from elders of a city all the way up to a king like David or Solomon, from punishing too harshly. This principle of not punishing beyond proportional justice is enshrined in the United States Constitution in the prohibition against "cruel and unusual punishment." The principle of "an eye for an eye" is especially aimed at preventing feuds between families and clans in ancient Israel. But feuding isn't just ancient;

the bloody feud between the Hatfield and the McCoy clans in West Virginia and Kentucky lasted from 1863 to 1891. Murderous feuding is still found between street gangs, a large factor in the recent spike in murder rates in some major American cities, where both gang members and innocent bystanders suffered violence.

Another important thing to note about "an eye for an eye" is that it's a legal proverb, not meant to be applied as a clear-cut law. In all the pages of the Old Testament, it was not carried out literally, except, of course, a "life for a life"; people were regularly put to death in ancient Israel for committing murder. There's no instance in the Old Testament of anyone, including city authorities responsible for the administration of justice, removing anyone's eye as a penalty. Neither is there any record of anyone losing a tooth, a hand, or a foot as a punishment for destroying a tooth, hand or foot of someone else. People were not burned or wounded for burning or wounding anyone. Instead, monetary fines were imposed, or if the crime was considered severe, criminals were either put to the lash or put to death for it. (Keep in mind that there were no prisons for long-term incarceration at this time.) In sum, the Old Testament advances a civilized system of proportional, reciprocal justice. The "eye-for-an-eye" principle of careful justice is summed up well in our saying "The punishment should fit the crime."

What does the corrected understanding of "an eye for an eye" mean for us today? First, when this principle is applied correctly in a system of proportional justice, wrongs are addressed and there is an end to violence. Gandhi was wrong about this; "an eye for an eye," when applied with Old Testament guidelines, doesn't make the whole world blind. Far from being barbaric, when the principle correctly applied it is a huge step forward in human life from uncontrolled vengeance and feuding. The proportional justice enshrined in "an eye for an eye" is still a basis of legal procedure today in most of the Western world. Jesus' replacing it for his followers with non-retaliation is an even bigger step forward, into the kingdom of God.

Second, we should ask, if this "eye-for-an-eye" principle is so effective, why did Jesus cancel it for his followers? Matthew 5:38–39 says: "You have heard that it was said, 'An eye for an eye and a tooth for a tooth.' But I say to you, Do not resist the one who is evil. But if anyone slaps you on the right cheek, turn to him the other also." Jesus wants his followers not to harbor a spirit of resentment. If someone does us wrong, we are to meet it by doing something good and right to them. This command for Christians not to retaliate against evil goes deep into the New Testament. For example, the Apostle Paul says in Romans 12:17–19, "Repay no one evil for evil . . . Beloved, never avenge yourselves, but leave it to the wrath of God, for it is written, 'Vengeance is mine, I will repay, says the Lord.'" In v. 14 of that chapter, Paul says, "Bless those who persecute you; bless and do not curse them." In 1 Thessalonians 5:15 Paul states, "See that no one repays anyone evil for evil, but always seek to do good to one another and to everyone." The foundation of this ethic in the New Testament is the call to follow the example of Christ. In his life, Jesus replaced "an eye for an eye" with nonretaliation against evil and violence. In his death, Jesus suffered righteously, and he was vindicated in his resurrection. Christians follow his example as God's new way to deal with wrong. This is one reason why the cross became the main symbol of Christianity soon after the New Testament was written.

Third, although Jesus' followers today give up this "eye-for-an-eye" principle in their own lives to follow a better way, does it have a place in God's will for the world in which we still live? Or to put it another way, does "an eye for an eye" have anything to offer us in our efforts to secure more justice in the world? I believe it does. In public life today, it is still a good principle of justice that punishment should fit the crime, that is, be proportional to the crime. When we move away from the basic idea that punishment should fit the crime, injustice results and crimes may increase. Sometimes a punishment is too light, as when in an infamous 2016 case a former student at Stanford University was sentenced to six months in jail for raping an unconscious woman, resulting in an national outcry. (He got an early release for "good behavior.")[1] A maximum sentence for murder in some European countries like Norway, even for multiple murders, is now around twenty years. Another incident of too-light punishment began in my neighborhood in 2013 when a man was killed crossing a street late at night. Two drivers were speeding, allegedly racing each other, when they each hit him. They stopped their cars, looked at him lying in the street, and sped off to hide from the police without calling an ambulance or reporting the accident. Despite breaking several laws and causing a death, they reached a plea deal in which they were sentenced to a few months in county jail and a few years of probation. This led to a loud public outcry over this injustice, and calls to change the laws. When human life is cheap, and justice is not done, God's purpose for human life is thwarted.

---

1. Fantz, "Outrage."

On the other hand, sometimes people may be punished too severely for crimes, as for example when people found with a small or moderate amount of certain drugs can be convicted of "possession with intent to sell" and sentenced to life in prison. (I'm not suggesting that this is not a serious crime, and I'm not implying that selling drugs is a nonviolent crime as some people claim, only that this punishment is perhaps too harsh.) Too-severe punishment also appeared in Victor Hugo's novel *Les Miserables*, when stealing a loaf of bread in the late 1700s led to a five-year prison term; the story is fictional, but the punishment is true to life. These harsh punishments would not be allowed under the Old Testament's "eye-for-an-eye" principle. Punishment that is too harsh removes some incentive for convicted people to change their lives, and can close off the possibility of restorative justice. In sum, when we say that the "punishment should fit the crime," we are affirming the continued place in our society of what the Bible actually means by "an eye for an eye."

QUESTIONS FOR REFLECTION AND DISCUSSION

1. What was your initial interpretation of "an eye for an eye?"
2. What is the principle being expressed in this verse?
3. Where do you see our society succeeding or failing in the principle of "the punishment should fit the crime"?
4. How does considering the genre of a biblical passage affect how we live it out? How does understanding the genre help us decide which biblical passages we should take literally and which we should not?
5. How does taking into consideration the whole witness of Scripture affect how we live out this Bible passage? Consider Matthew 5:38–39 and 1 Thessalonians 5:14–15.
6. Examine your own life in the light of this study. When do you find the desire for vengeance and paying back evil for evil rising up in yourself? How do you respond to that desire?

5

How Prosperous Does God Want Us to Be?

Then you shall make your way prosperous, and then you shall have good success. (Joshua 1:8)

PERHAPS YOU HAVE HEARD the following declaration: "If you name it and claim it in faith, God will give it. That's in the Bible." Or someone has said to you something like this: "You are still sick because you don't have enough faith. God wants you healthy." Or this, drawing on Joshua 1:8: "If you believe God's promise and affirm it, he will make you prosperous and successful."

Some Christians strongly maintain that God wants us to be financially prosperous, physically healthy, and otherwise successful in this life. This "health-and-wealth gospel," which is also called the "gospel of success" or (most often by its adherents) the "prosperity gospel," is prominent in North America today. If you watch religious programs on Sunday morning television, you will see it. The prosperity gospel has now spread widely to some Protestant churches in Asia and Africa, especially in independent, nondenominational churches. It maintains that physical health and financial wealth are always the will of God for Christians. Faith in this divine will, positive speech about it, and generous giving are said to increase one's material wealth greatly. The promise of the prosperity gospel for human health was summed up by televangelist Kenneth Hagin, one of its founders, "I am fully convinced—I would die saying it is so—that it is the plan of Our Father God, in His great love and in His great mercy, that no believer should ever be sick; that every believer should live his full life span down here on this earth; and that every believer should finally just fall asleep in Jesus."[1] Hagin and others have said similar things about wealth: God's will is that we should have plenty of it, and it should always increase.

Alongside the so-called prosperity gospel, there is a very different message in the Bible, about the spiritual dangers of prosperity to the people of God. Of course, gaining wealth does not automatically mean that people are disobedient to God or in spiritual danger. However, wealth can be detrimental to the faith and obedience of any prosperous Christian, and "pride in riches" is described as a main type of godlessness in 1 John 2:16. Which is correct, that wealth is a blessing or wealth is a danger? This large issue is admittedly a complex one that cannot be fully examined here. The main questions we will ask while examining Joshua 1:8 are these: How prosperous does God want us to be? And what do "prosperous" and "successful" really mean? As we will see, it is a misunderstanding of this and other "prosperity" verses to think that they promise health and wealth to individual Christians today.

Before we consider Joshua 1:8, we should examine its context. In Joshua 1:1–6, God commands Joshua to act with courage and confidence in preparing the people to enter their new land. The passage continues:

> 7 Only be strong and very courageous, being careful to do according to all the law which Moses my servant commanded you; turn not from it to the right hand or to the left, that you may have good success wherever you go. 8 This book of the law shall not depart out of your mouth, but you shall meditate on it day and night, that you may be careful to do according to all that is written in it; for then you shall make your way prosperous, and then you shall have good success. 9 Have I not commanded you? Be strong and of good courage; be not frightened, neither be dismayed; for the LORD your God is with you wherever you go. (RSV)

Much of the prosperity gospel's view of financial prosperity as God's blessing is based on passages like this in the Bible, which seem to promise financial prosperity and success to those who obey God. (See, among many others, Malachi 3:10 ["bring the tithes" into God's storehouse for abundant blessing], Jeremiah 29:11 [God has "plans to prosper you"], John 10:10 [Jesus came so his followers would have life "abundantly"], and James 4:2 ["You do not have because you do not ask."].) The context of Joshua 1:8 makes clear that this is a misunderstanding. The prosperity of Israel as a

---

1. Hagin, *Seven Things You Should Know*, 21.

whole in the promised land is in view here, not prosperity for each individual, then or today. "Success" in vv. 7 and 8 is not a general or personal success, but in this context it means being successful in conquering and holding the promised land (see especially "wherever you go" in v. 7). This promise of success is a motivation for the leaders and people of Israel to "be strong and courageous" in the face of battles to come, an admonition repeated often in Joshua 1:1–9. Being successful is directly linked with keeping the laws that God gave the Israelites through Moses. In this verse and generally in the Old Testament, obedience leads to continued flourishing of the people of God in the land that God has given them. Preachers of the prosperity gospel typically do not emphasize this theme of obedience to God in all of life as a condition of divine blessing.

It's safe to say that God wants all people to have the necessary resources to sustain life at a basic level. For billions of poor people in the world today, even a little movement toward prosperity would be a blessing. The prosperity gospel is correct about that. But we need to hear the strong countervoice in the Bible about the dangers of wealth. Wealth is understood in the Bible as having much more than what one needs for basic daily life. The temptation to become affluent, and the ever-increasing prosperity that many prosperity gospel preachers talk about, can lead to sin. It can lead to exploitation of the poor, for instance depriving them of their rightful wages. It can lead to the temptation to steal, whether pilfering or embezzling from one's employer or defrauding one's clients. It can also lead to men and women neglecting their spouses, families, and churches in order to work long hours in starting a new business or otherwise trying to make big money. In 2015, for example, a public controversy broke out over the announcement that the newly appointed head of the Yahoo technology company, who was pregnant with twins, would work through her upcoming two-week maternity leave.[2] Some worried that her prominent example would harm the ability of women and men to take family leave. I've known professors who work ten or more hours a day at their jobs, often seven days a week, to build a record that will get them tenure and promotion. Attorneys trying to become partners in their firms are known to work even harder. To be fair, though, we should acknowledge that working long hours is not always for the purpose of accumulating wealth. Some people must work at two or more jobs just to make enough money to support their families at a basic level.

---

2. Walters, "Yahoo CEO."

The worst temptation of wealth, in the Bible's view, is that it often undermines faith and dependence on God. The Bible itself warns that the prosperity God gave to Israel could lead to a loss of faith. For example, Deuteronomy 8:11–14a says, "Take care that you do not forget the Lord your God, by failing to keep his commandments, his ordinances, and his statutes, which I am commanding you today. When you have eaten your fill and have built fine houses and live in them, and when your herds and flocks have multiplied, and your silver and gold is multiplied, and all that you have is multiplied, then do not exalt yourself, forgetting the Lord your God." This loss of faith and obedience leads in turn to all sorts of evils that the Old Testament prophets regularly denounce: idolatry, murder, sexual sins, theft, and others. An excellent attitude to riches and poverty is eloquently taught in Proverbs 30:8–9, a passage typically ignored by preachers of the prosperity gospel: "Give me neither poverty nor riches. Feed me with the food that is necessary for me, lest I be full and deny you, and say, 'Who is the Lord?' or lest I be poor and steal, and profane the name of my God." This should be the prayer of Christians tempted by the prosperity gospel.

Where most Christians disagree with the prosperity gospel is in its peculiar understanding of Isaiah 53:5, "by his stripes we are healed." This is a key text in the Christian doctrine of salvation when it was applied by the first Christians to Jesus' death. The prosperity gospel uses this expression to promise physical healing to every Christian who has enough faith; it is one of this movement's most important texts. The vast majority of church tradition has always interpreted Isaiah 53:5 as a metaphor referring to salvation. The Bible does not otherwise teach that physical healing is provided in the atonement. Dozens of passages do explicitly teach that our sin has been forgiven through Christ's death, and some have implications about the physical healing that resurrection will bring at the re-creation of the world. However, no text explicitly says the same about physical healing in this life, not Isaiah 53:5 or even its uses in the New Testament. The atonement worked by Christ on the cross was not to establish a prosperity gospel that guarantees us physical health.

Several Christian economists have studied the prosperity gospel's ideas and given broad reasons to reject them. We can summarize them here as an important perspective on this issue.[3] First, the prosperity gospel undermines the relationship between work and well-being. God's design for human life has always included labor, even before the fall (Genesis 2:15).

---

3. This summary is drawn from Spencer, "Prosperity Gospel."

After the fall, God made work harder (Genesis 3:17–19), but God still intends for people to work for their sustenance and well-being (2 Thessalonians 3:10–12). Second, many Christian economists say that the prosperity gospel undermines efforts to bring people out of poverty. Arguing that simply believing in the prosperity gospel will fix the problem of poverty for individuals ignores systemic problems or the need for the poor to acquire new skills and habits. Third, the prosperity gospel can make church members who are poor or sick feel guilty, and their faith is threatened, when they are told that their lack of belief is to blame for their troubles. Fourth, the prosperity gospel militates against spiritual contentment, because it teaches that faith must always receive a fresh injection of wealth from God.

The prosperity gospel does get some things right. God did create this world as a rich place, a wonderful home for humanity. The richness of the earth should lead to some measure of prosperity for all people, so that all have basic food, clothing, shelter, and medical care. In regard to healing, most Christians would agree with some teachings in the prosperity gospel, if not with its entire system. For example, recognizing that the physical body is God's creation may lead to better care for the body, and thus to a measure of better overall physical health. Also, the healing of human life is part of our salvation. Miracles of healing were an important part of the ministry of Jesus, the apostles, and the early church—and not just to attract attention and get a hearing for the good news. When God does heal someone, it is a sign that the kingdom of God is already at work in the present. Christians have always prayed for the sick with an expectation of some level of healing. In the big picture, God does desire the wholeness and flourishing of all people and all creation, and eventually God will make all of that come around right.

What are the implications of a corrected understanding of this verse for Christians today? First, it has a direct bearing on our attitude as we give to God. Giving should be a matter of expressing thankfulness to God. The same is true about obedience; it should be an expression of gratitude, not a way to claim a personal benefit from God. However, some Christians who believe in the prosperity gospel give, and in particular tithe, in order to persuade or even obligate God to make them more prosperous. This idea can even be heard occasionally in Protestant churches that don't subscribe to the prosperity gospel. It may be appropriate for church leaders to encourage Christians, "Give in faith, trusting that God will provide for your needs." But saying "If you give to God, you will get much more from God" tempts hearers to become greedy and implies that a relationship with

God is based on a financial contract, not on humble faith. Living under the prosperity gospel is a bit like playing the lottery: one invests a little money in God, hoping that God will multiply it and that one will end up with a much larger amount.

Second, we should seek stability in our basic needs, but seeking to be wealthy is a trap today just as much as it was in New Testament times: "Those who want to be rich fall into temptation and are trapped by many senseless and harmful desires that plunge people into ruin and destruction" (1 Timothy 6:9). If God gives us prosperity, a prosperity honestly gained, it is our duty to be generous with it. Ephesians 4:28 puts it well: "Let the thief no longer steal, but rather let him labor, doing honest work with his own hands." The reason given here for honest work is not rooted in a prosperity gospel, that the former thief can become financially well-off and feel God's ever-increasing blessing. Rather, the reason for honest work—all honest work, we might add, not just by repentant thieves—is that we "may have something to share with those in need." That's what the real "prosperity gospel" is all about.

QUESTIONS FOR REFLECTION AND DISCUSSION

1. Reflect on this thought-provoking statement to middle-and-upper class Americans by Elisabeth Elliot: *"God has promised to supply all our needs. What we don't have now, we don't need now."*
2. One of the main factors enabling the rise of irreligiousness is widespread prosperity in a society. What does this say about a common understanding of the Christian faith?
3. How does the Bible's understanding of being wealthy and having success differ from ours today? What difference does that make in understanding this topic?
4. If you look carefully at yourself, can you identify your real motives for giving? What are they?
5. An advertisement some years ago pitched "luxury necessities." Is there such a thing? What is the line between luxury and necessity?
6. What might be the result of framing success and prosperity as characterizing a group (for example, the church) rather than an individual?

6

How Do We Hide God's Word in Our Hearts?

I have hidden your word in my heart that I might not sin against you. (Psalm 119:11)

IF YOU GREW UP in the Christian faith, you may have memorized Bible verses when you were a child. Bible memorization is an important part of Christian education, especially in Protestant Sunday schools. Children learn verses like John 3:16 from an early age, and they keep on learning short Bible verses at least through elementary school years. But Bible memorization is not just for children. Many evangelical Protestant churches urge Bible memorization for all their members. The late Christian philosopher Dallas Willard wrote, "I would never undertake to pastor a church or guide a program of Christian education that did not involve a continuous program of memorization of the choicest passages of Scripture for people of all ages."[1]

Psalm 119:11 is one of the main verses said to be about the importance of Bible memorization. In fact, it's the verse in the Bible that seems to speak most directly about it. As a result, it is often quoted to emphasize the importance of Bible memorization: "I have hidden your word in my heart that I might not sin against you" (Psalm 119:11, NIV). This verse has become very familiar to many Christians. Unfortunately, it is often misunderstood

1. Willard, *Spirit of the Disciplines*, 150.

How Do We Hide God's Word in Our Hearts?

and misused. The misunderstanding is two-part, and begins with this. For us today, to learn something "by heart" means to memorize it. When we use "heart" this way, we really mean "mind": we can say it from memory. This is why the *American Heritage Dictionary* can define the expression "by heart" as "learned by rote, memorized word for word." It's in our mind and we can repeat it to ourselves, as when we know a poem or hymn "by heart." So the first misunderstanding of this verse is confusing "heart" for "mind," and thinking that this verse is speaking of memorization in the mind. A second misunderstanding is the idea that if we have internalized Scripture we will necessarily be obedient to God. Memorizing God's word is believed to lead to doing God's will more fully. We can know better what is right and wrong in God's sight by knowing the Bible, and knowing it can help us avoid sin. That may be true—we will consider it further below—but is it what *this verse* means?

To answer this question, let's look first at the context of this idea in the Old Testament as a whole. The writer of Psalm 119 draws on Deuteronomy 6:6 and 30:14, where the people of God put God's law "on/in the heart." One short section of Proverbs 3:1, 3 is a sort of parallel passage to Psalm 119:11, and it can also shed light on the expression "hide in my heart." Here a father, teaching God's wisdom to his son, says, "My son, do not forget my teaching, but keep my commands in your heart . . . Let love and faithfulness never leave you; bind them around your neck, and write them on the tablet of your heart." (In the ancient Near East, students had small slate tablets on which they wrote with chalk.) In Psalm 119:11 we see the same idea that keeping God's commands in our heart, and writing them there, is a necessary part of wise obedience to God. Note that "heart" is used here consistently, not "mind" or "understanding."

Now we should look at the context of this single verse in Psalm 119. Most Christians who know anything about the size of the book of Psalms know that 119 is the longest. It is also the only psalm that is alphabetic in form. In each section every verse begins with a particular letter of the Hebrew alphabet; the first section begins with *aleph*, the second with *beth*, all the way through the twenty-two letters of the Hebrew alphabet. This structure makes its content a bit disjointed. The effect that the compiler of this psalm seems to be aiming for could be called "Wisdom from A to Z." Despite being long and disjointed, this psalm has a thematic unity around the idea of loving and keeping God's word, and it has a poetic beauty that can only be appreciated by "living in" this psalm for an extended time. The words of v. 11 are echoed in other verses of this psalm. For example, in vv. 111–12 we read, "Your statutes are my heritage forever; they are the joy of my heart. My heart is set on keeping your decrees to the very end." Verse 167 states, "I obey your statutes, for I love them greatly." And in v. 104 is the important "flip side" of this love, rejection of what God says is wrong, which the psalmist calls "hatred" of evil. The context of the whole psalm clearly shows that not just memorizing is important, but meditating on God's word is important too. Only a strong love for God's commandments will lead to a commitment to keeping them.

We are now in a position to look at this verse itself. A careful reading shows that it does not suggest that memorizing the Bible *in itself* will lead us to be better Christians. This is a common idea among some Protestants. For example, the American pastor Robert J. Morgan said this about memorizing the Bible: "It's vital for mental and emotional health and for spiritual well-being . . . It allows God's words to sink into your brain and permeate your subconscious thoughts. It saturates the personality, satiates the soul, and stockpiles the mind. It changes the atmosphere of every family and alters the weather forecast of every day."[2] Even after accounting for poetic exaggeration, this claims too much for memorization. Thinking that memorizing Bible verses will lead in itself to a changed, more Christian character is a common misunderstanding. What is more important is to work the word of God from our minds into our hearts. In the Old Testament, the "heart" is primarily the seat of the will or motivation, and secondarily a place of thought and memory. Both often go together in the Bible, but the motivational meaning is primary. This can be seen in vv. 111–12 just quoted above, in which the heart is full of joy over God's commandments, and this joyful heart is "set on keeping [God's] decrees." In the Bible's view, we do think with our hearts, but, even more, we form intentions with them.

Another key point is the meaning of the word "hide." It doesn't mean "keep secret" inside one's mind, which is our usual understanding today, and a part of the misunderstanding of this verse. Instead, some recent Bible translations, such as the NRSV, say "treasure," not "hide." The Hebrew word for "to hide" here is used around thirty times in the Old Testament, and does have the primary meaning of "hide" or "store," which is why most Bible translations render it as "hidden" in Psalm 119:11. It comes to have a deeper meaning of "to treasure," since hiding was what one often did with valuables in the days before there were banks. So when the psalmist says,

---

2. Morgan, *100 Bible Verses*, xiii.

"Your word have I hidden in my heart," he means that the word is being hidden and stored up there as something valuable—like a treasure.

Those who misunderstand this verse have some things correct about it. They know that God's word is a good thing. It is good for us simply because it is God's word, not ours. They also know that God has revealed his word to us, and that we can keep it in our minds and hearts. They are correct that pastors and teachers of the Bible should encourage its memorization as a part of growth in the Christian faith.

What is the significance of the corrected meaning of this verse? First, memorizing the Bible can be overvalued. It won't by itself produce greater obedience to God. Knowing the word of God doesn't automatically lead to doing it; only treasuring it may lead to obeying it. A striking example of knowing the Bible while not living it is provided by Nikita Khrushchev, the leader of the Soviet Union in the 1960s. As a boy in czarist Russia, he won a Bible memorizing contest at his local Russian Orthodox church, and in his adult years as an atheist he frequently quoted the Bible for his own political purposes, much to the astonishment of other communists. God wants the Word to sink deeper than the memory in our minds, to sink all the way into our hearts, shaping our deepest emotions and our strongest intentions. Of course, to be treasured in our hearts, it has to be there, and one of the best ways to begin to get God's word into our hearts is to memorize it.

Second, the Bible reminds us that knowing, even treasuring God's will doesn't guarantee our doing it. Psalm 119 acknowledges with the rest of the Old Testament that sin is ever-present for all people, and this would include those with the Bible in their minds and hearts. This sober reality is strengthened in the New Testament, which takes a realistic view of how prone to sin we humans really are, even as Christians. It isn't any good to know the word of God if we don't do it. Jesus implies this when he tells his disciples, "If you know these things, blessed are you if you do them" (John 13:17), and doing the will of God instead of just hearing it is a leading theme in the Letter of James (1:22–27). Even *wanting* to do something doesn't mean we will do it, as the apostle Paul reminds us: "What I want to do I do not do, but what I hate, I do" (Romans 7:15). Most Christians today, if they are honest with themselves, can confess to a similar experience. Evil is not just a state of mind that among other things causes us to forget God's commandments. Paul knows that it has a power that can overcome our knowledge of what God wants and our good intentions to do it.

Third, given the power of sin, Christians must rely on the Holy Spirit's power within them to know and do what is right. The Spirit's power comes not only at holy times such as conversion or baptism; it also comes as a process, leading believers to "put on" what is good and to "put off" what is evil. For all Christians, this process is not meant to be easy, and it's never as easy as simply memorizing the Bible. Does this mean that hiding God's word in us is useless? Not at all. But because of the New Testament's realistic depiction of the spiritual warfare of the Christian life, our treasuring the word of God should be even stronger—and more Spirit-directed—than the psalmist could have imagined.

QUESTIONS FOR REFLECTION AND DISCUSSION

1. What have been your past experiences with memorizing Scripture?
2. What are some memorized passages that have been particularly meaningful to you? How have they affected the way you live?
3. How can we get the word beyond just our minds, into our hearts?
4. What are the implications of the fact that "hide" in this passage suggests "treasure"? Does the word seem like treasure to us? Why or why not?
5. How does knowing the word of God without doing it lead to self-deception? What might be dangerous about it?
6. What role does the Holy Spirit play in the way we live the Christian life?

7

Is "Train Up a Child" a Promise?

Train up a child in the way he should go, and when he is old he will not depart from it. (Proverbs 22:6)

MOST CHRISTIAN PARENTS WANT to raise their children in the Christian faith. Until about fifty years ago, parents could generally count on the wider North American culture—schools, businesses, government, and so forth—to reinforce Christian values, or at least not to oppose them. This helped to keep the children of Christians in the faith when they grew up. Today, North American culture doesn't reinforce church life or Christian values. In fact, it often presses against them. North America is increasingly irreligious, and young people in their teens and twenties are especially vulnerable to the pressures of irreligion. A growing feature of life in North America is open hostility to the Christian faith and church. A striking illustration of this comes from a colleague who is a regional denominational administrator in the Northeast, who said that non-Christians in his region often think that churches are dangerous organizations, full of hypocrisy, greed, and sexual abuse. As a result, people in his area who go to church can be looked on with suspicion by people who don't. This hostility, where it occurs, makes raising our children in the faith even harder.

The title of John Westerhoff's book, *Will Our Children Have Faith?*, is even more pointed now than when he wrote this book in 1976.[1] Of course,

---

1. Westerhoff, *Will Our Children Have Faith?*

young people have been opting out of church for generations. What's new is the size of the problem, which has been growing since the 1960s. Young people in North America leave our churches today more than ever before: estimates vary between 40 and 70 percent. Most of the young people who leave do not come back, although some return when they themselves have children. When so many young people leave the church, the membership numbers of churches are bound to be affected. North American and European mainline denominations, with their relatively low birth rates and low rates of conversions, are in trouble over the long term if they can't keep their children in the faith.

The departure of children from the faith causes pain to Christian parents. One parent whose children have left the church told me that he has never prayed as hard for his children as when they gave up the church, and his pain grew much worse when his grandchildren were not raised as Christians. In the face of the loss of our children from the faith, many Christian parents cling tightly to Proverbs 22:6: "Train up a child in the way he should go, and when he is old he will not depart from it." They understand this verse to be the Bible's promise that if they raise their children in the faith, this training will stick, and they will stay in the faith through their adult years. There's no such thing as a perfect parent, but this verse doesn't say that only perfect parents can instill faith in their children. Many people today see it as a clear guarantee, an ironclad promise: Do your best to train your child in God's way, and God will bless this effort by keeping your children in this way all through their lives. Counselors and family therapists who practice from an evangelical Protestant stance have often made this understanding of Proverbs 22:6 a key part of their practice.[2]

However, is this really a guarantee, or a guideline offering general results? In other words, is it a promise or a proverb? Like most wise sayings in the Bible, this is a general principle, and is worded that way. It's not an absolute guarantee, as if we can obligate God to keep our children faithful by raising them correctly. This verse is in fact a proverb, and to interpret it as a more or less absolute promise is to misunderstand it. Biblical proverbs are not promises. Rather, they are brief expressions of a general truth with the possibility of exceptions. An important part of training in wisdom in ancient Israel was to understand how proverbs worked (Proverbs 1:1–7), which involved knowing how a particular proverb applied and how it didn't. (We do the same thing today with our proverbs. For example, we

---

2. See Schultz, *Out of Context*, 96–97.

say "Look before you leap," but we also say "He who hesitates is lost," and we must apply these opposite proverbs correctly.) In short, to use Proverbs 22:6 as a guarantee of lifelong success as parents is to misapply it.

The main misunderstanding of this verse comes in its second half: "when he is old, he will not depart from it." It's easy to interpret this as guarantee, or at least a strong promise, because it seems to be the obvious meaning of the text. But this is a mistake because the misunderstanding ignores that this verse is a proverb and that a proverb's purpose is to give broad, general advice and point to broad results. As a general expectation, it is accurate enough to say that many children raised in the faith will likely keep to it. At least they have the opportunity to keep to it, because they were raised in it. But to expect that *all* children raised in the faith will stay in it is to ignore what the Bible says about individual responsibility to keep the faith, and the responsibility of every child raised in the faith to affirm it personally and live in it.

On what basis do believers raise their children to be faithful Christians? Should we hold God to a promise here in this verse, or hold this promise to be an ironclad guarantee? Or, conversely, if our children give up the faith as adults, should we automatically conclude that we have done a bad job in raising them? This would in many cases not be an accurate or fair judgment, but some Christian parents have suffered unnecessary guilt and grief for it. Instead, we must recognize the fact, as the Bible from the first page to the last, that people are responsible for their own choices in life. As the prophet Jeremiah said to Israel, all individuals are responsible for their own choices to serve God. They can't complain that "the parents have eaten sour grapes, and the children's teeth are set on edge," in an effort to blame their sin on their parents (Jeremiah 31:29–30). Young people must make their own choices, and we can't compel our children to stay in the faith, much as we would like to. Even God, the best parent of all, had his children Adam and Eve depart from his way and turn to their own path.

Do people who misunderstand this verse have anything correct about it? They do, especially in the first half of the verse. They correctly see it as a command to raise children in God's way. The first part of the verse is an imperative in Hebrew, and hence a command, and it is translated that way in most English versions. Most of them correctly understand that in the context of Proverbs and the Bible in general, "the way" refers to the way of life that God reveals to his people. A few interpreters of this verse say that "in the way he should go," refers to a child's specific "way" suited to her or his individual personality and particular traits. This, they say, is the course that a child will not leave. Suiting the Christian training of our children to their personality is indeed a good idea, but this verse isn't referring to that. "Way" in the Bible, including in Proverbs, does not refer to an individualized path of life, but to the main path of faith and obedience that God has laid down for all.

Three main takeaways for Christian life today arise from the corrected view of this verse. First, "training up children in the way they should go" is still a wise and necessary thing. God commands us to train our children in the way they should go even though there are no ironclad guarantees about the result. One of the most important passages of the Old Testament deals with raising one's children in the faith: "Impress [these words] on your children. Talk about them when you sit at home and when you walk along the road, when you lie down and when you get up" (Deuteronomy 6:7). Only if successive generations of the people of Israel lived faithfully with God would it go well with them as God continued to bless them (Deuteronomy 12:28; 30:16). This obedience to God through the generations clearly entails raising children in the faith, but it also entails each generation's taking on the responsibility of serving God. Protestants may differ on how ceremonially we show that our children belong to God (are they to be baptized or dedicated?), but all practicing Protestants see training their children to love God and walk in God's way as necessary.

The increasing irreligiousness of North American life today makes raising children in the faith all the more a necessity, but more difficult as well. A number of Christian parents today say, "We'll let our children make their own choices about religion when they grow up," supposing this is a good thing to do. This verse reminds us that God expects us to train children to walk in the way of faith; neutrality to God is not an option. The Israelite male "child" of Proverbs 22:6 was without doubt circumcised in the covenant and raised in it. For a Christian today, it is no more possible to raise children to be neutral to God than it is to raise them to be neutral to right and wrong. A joke making the rounds recently made clever fun of this false neutrality. It describes a mother and a visitor in a living room watching two little children crawling on all fours and snarling at each other with teeth bared. The mother says to the concerned visitor, "I'm Catholic and my husband is Protestant, so we're raising our children as wolves." All humor aside, this unwillingness to pass on the faith to children has an impact on the life of the church and its leadership, an impact that goes beyond numbers. Alister McGrath, a leading British theologian, recently stated that one of the most significant current challenges in the education of people for ordained Christian ministry is dealing with the failure of the church and Christian parents to pass on knowledge of the faith to the next generation. Even when the faith is passed on, he says, careful knowledge of it is not, and young people come to higher education for ministry not having the foundation they need.

Second, this verse invites us to mull over the wise sayings of Proverbs and think deeply about them. "Claiming a promise" in the book of Proverbs that may or may not be there is not appropriate. The proverbs look short and simple, but usually they aren't. Instead, the still waters of the proverbs run deep. Wrestling with the meaning of this verse, and learning how it applies and when it does not apply, will do us and our children good.

Third, all I've said here brings me to a word of caution for those parents whose children stay in the faith: Don't claim too much personal credit for it. Just as children who leave the faith do so by their own decision, so too children who stay in the faith do so by their own decision. Of course, parents whose children stay in the faith are rightly happy about this. But pride or self-congratulation should have no place in them. Instead, they should be humbly grateful to God.

QUESTIONS FOR REFLECTION AND DISCUSSION

1. What can the church do better to keep more of its children in the faith?
2. Some see a promise in Proverbs 22:6, that if their children leave the faith, they will come back at some point. What do you think about this expectation?
3. What does it feel like for parents when children leave the faith? What is the difference between leaving the faith and leaving a certain congregation or denomination?
4. Is a child leaving "the way he should go" an automatic indication that parents have done something wrong? Have you ever been tempted toward that sort of judgment of yourself or others?
5. How can those of us in the church support parents whose grown children have left the faith?

6. A popular current expression for Christian commitment that lasts through the generations is "sticky faith." What do you think about this expression?

8

The End of the World or the Beginning of a New World?

For I am about to create new heavens and a new earth. (Isaiah 65:17)

A POPULAR QUESTION USED in evangelism as an opening to a conversation has been, "If you died today, would you go to heaven?"[1] Some Christians wonder if this is a good way to open a conversation about evangelism—after all, one doesn't see such a question used in the New Testament, and it could be off-putting to some. It does, however, raise the important issue of how we view eternity, and this view in turn shapes the way we believe and live today.

Most misunderstood verses of the Bible get that way because they are taken out of context and given a new meaning. Sometimes they are misunderstood in a second way, when people realize only a part of their meaning, as with John 3:16 or the parable of the Good Samaritan. The verse covered in this chapter is misunderstood for a third reason: Christians have such strong views on a topic that Bible passages challenging those views are simply ignored, or their meanings are twisted around to suit one's views. A prominent example of this third type of misunderstanding is the Christian doctrine of what happens at the "end of the world," a topic known more formally as the "last things." Many Christians believe that the "end of the world" is literally that—at the end of time, the world will be destroyed

---

1. See, for example, Kennedy, *Evangelism Explosion*, 35.

and stay that way forever. After the last judgment, they also believe, God's people will go to heaven, their new home, where they will live a mostly spiritual existence. We can put the two contrasting views of the last things in this way: Will the future bring the permanent end of this world and the transfer of God's people to a mysterious place called heaven, or will it bring the coming of a new world in which heaven and earth are re-created and unified? Although it is surprising to many North American Christians today, the second view is what the Bible teaches.

Here is an illustration of how surprising the Bible's promise of new heaven and new earth can be. When I was teaching on this topic a few years ago to my New Testament introduction class, I stressed that the Christian's eternal home is not in heaven, but in a new, re-created heaven and on a new, re-created earth. I pointed out how this aligns with the teaching of Jesus on the kingdom of God, with the letters of Paul and Peter, and with the visions of Revelation. One of my students grew increasingly agitated as this point went on. Finally he couldn't contain himself any longer, and as his hand shot up he blurted out, "But doesn't 2 Peter 3:12 say that the earth will be destroyed by fire?" Sensing a teachable moment, I asked him to find the verse after the one he had quoted and read it out loud for the class, which he did: "But according to God's promise we are looking for new heavens and a new earth, in which righteousness dwells." A sheepish look came over his face, and he said, "Oh, I guess I didn't notice that." I replied, "You aren't alone. Many Christians think that this world will be destroyed forever, and that's the end of it. Instead, we will live righteous lives in the new heavens and on the new earth."

The Christian doctrine of the last things has its deep roots in the Old Testament, where it was one of the last major doctrines to develop. When prophets in ancient Israel began to speak about what we call the last things, they didn't prophesy that the world would be destroyed and all the faithful go off to heaven and live there in God's home. Neither did they say that the last things are accomplished as the people of God die and go one by one to heaven. Instead, they prophesied a different vision that they received from God, a vision for a new heaven and new earth, a complete new creation as a home for a fully redeemed, fully obedient humanity. Some of the details of the Bible's view of the future changed as God revealed more about the last things, but the main initial vision of new heavens and a new earth endured and became foundational for the whole teaching. Eternity will see humankind on a restored earth fully connected to heaven, not removed to God's

The End of the World or the Beginning of a New World? 53

heavenly realm. Human history reaches its culmination, and the full reign of God is realized, where it all began, here on the earth.

A close look at Isaiah 65:17 in its context bears this out. In Isaiah 65:13–15 we have alternating promises of blessings for God's faithful people and shame and pain for the rebellious. This will become important in the last verse of Isaiah 66, which we will deal with below. Verse 16 contains an affirmation of God's faithfulness. Then comes our passage, beginning in v. 17. God says these things through the prophet:

> 17 "See, I will create
>   new heavens and a new earth.
> The former things will not be remembered,
>   nor will they come to mind.
> 18 But be glad and rejoice forever
>   in what I will create,
> for I will create Jerusalem to be a delight
>   and its people a joy.
> 19 I will rejoice over Jerusalem
>   and take delight in my people;
> the sound of weeping and of crying
>   will be heard in it no more.
>
> 20 Never again will there be in it
>   an infant who lives but a few days,
> or an old man who does not live out his years;
> the one who dies at a hundred
>   will be thought a mere child;
> the one who fails to reach a hundred
>   will be considered accursed.
> 21 They will build houses and dwell in them;
>   they will plant vineyards and eat their fruit.
> 22 No longer will they build houses and others live in them,
>   or plant and others eat . . .
> 23 They will not labor in vain,
>   nor will they bear children doomed to misfortune;
> for they will be a people blessed by the Lord,
>   they and their descendants with them.
> 24 Before they call I will answer;
>   while they are still speaking I will hear.
> 25 The wolf and the lamb will feed together,
>   and the lion will eat straw like the ox,
> and dust will be the serpent's food.

> They will neither harm nor destroy
> on all my holy mountain,"
> says the Lord. (NIV)

We now should take a closer look at this famous passage. First and foremost, note that Isaiah 65:17–25 is shaped throughout by the "new heavens-and-new-earth" idea it opens with. This is the first time this expression appears in Scripture, and this full statement explains it well. The coming of new heavens and new earth is so momentous that the verb "create" is used, the same Hebrew word as in Genesis 1:1. This re-creation will cause all the shortcomings and evils of the old world to be utterly forgotten (v. 17). Its announcement should bring great joy even now to the people of God (vv. 18–19). God will take "delight in my people"; they will not cry any longer as they did in the old world (v. 19), a thought echoed in Revelation 7:17: "God will wipe away every tear from their eyes." Verse 20 of this passage may be a bit puzzling to us: long life is promised to all God's people in this re-created world, but not eternal life; the knowledge of that is still to come in the Old Testament. Another possibly puzzling aspect is the Jerusalem-centered re-creation envisioned here; the re-creation of the whole world is envisioned in this passage, but Jerusalem has a special place in it. This idea will continue all the way to the end of the New Testament, where John sees the "new Jerusalem" coming down from heaven (Revelation 21:1–2). In all their life in the new heavens and the new earth, God's people will be fully blessed (v. 23b). When they pray, God will hear them and respond immediately, even before they ask (v. 24); Jesus echoes this in his teaching on faithful prayer (Matthew 6:8). Even the world of nature will be at peace. Previously hostile animals will coexist with one another (v. 25), and the "peaceable kingdom" of Eden will be restored. In sum, this passage doesn't match fully what most Jews and Christians would later believe about the last things (judgment of all people, eternal life, and so forth), but it does lay a firm foundation for it.

The other occurrence of "new heavens and new earth" comes in the last verses of the book of Isaiah, 66:22–24. We should examine it briefly:

> 22 "As the new heavens and the new earth that I make will endure before me," declares the Lord, "so will your name and descendants endure. 23 From one New Moon to another and from one Sabbath to another, all mankind will come and bow down before me," says the Lord. 24 "And they will go out and look on the dead bodies of those who rebelled against me; the worms that eat them will not

die, the fire that burns them will not be quenched, and they will be loathsome to all mankind." (NIV)

This passage begins by affirming what chapter 65 already said about Israel's new hope: the new heavens and new earth will endure forever, and the people of God will endure in it (v. 22). Then comes something new: people from around the earth will come into God's presence and worship God (v. 23); this may imply that they will be made a part of the people of God. This finds a strong echo in Revelation's visions of the end, especially in its chapter 21, where "new heavens and new earth," populated by people from the whole earth, lead off the final, glorious vision of the consummation of all things.

But this glorious, harmonious note is not the way the long symphony of Isaiah ends. A somber final prophecy rings out in 66:24 in a way that seems jarring to many people today, about the punishment of the wicked who have resisted God's way. The blessed residents of the re-created world, probably meant as the New Jerusalem here, will gaze on an awful sight, the unburied bodies of those who refused God's way, the "many" that God has slain (Isaiah 66:16). Isaiah says about these bodies, "The worms that eat them will not die, the fire that burns them will not be quenched, and they will be loathsome to all mankind." This gruesome picture is a difficult way to end a prophetic book, particularly one as hopeful as Isaiah. (When this passage is read in many Jewish synagogue services, the reader goes back and reads again some happier verses from these two chapters.) The enduring quality of the new earth applies also to God's punishment of the wicked. The images of v. 24, the worms and the fire, are used by Jesus when he describes eternal punishment in Mark 9:48. These images, particularly the fire, played a large role in how Christians have imagined hell.

What takeaways for Christians today come from the corrected understanding of this passage? First, we must point out that this passage speaks about the final state of the re-created world, and the final state of the people of God in it. But Christians have been asking from the middle of the first century, what about the period between the death of the believer and the re-creation of heaven and earth when Jesus returns? Isaiah does not address it, of course, so we must look farther into the Bible for it. In the New Testament, belief in what is called the "intermediate state" begins. As Paul contemplates his death before the coming of Jesus, he says that it will bring him into the presence of Christ, and this has a strong appeal to him (Philippians 1:23). Although Paul is speaking only of himself here, Christians have rightly seen this to be true of all who belong to Christ. In 1 Thessalonians 4:13–18, Paul says that God will bring with Jesus, when he returns, all believers who have died: he will bring them with him because they are with him now. Very few details are given about this intermediate state of blessing, other than that it is a blessed life with Jesus. As the New Testament scholar N. T. Wright has written, this is "life after death" for Christians, but this is not at all the end of God's plan for eternal life. "Life after life after death," to use Wright's expression, is life in the new heavens and new earth. This is more important by far, even though many Christians focus their hope on "life after death" rather than on "life after life after death."[2] We don't wait until cosmic re-creation to be with Christ, because the bond that Christ has forged with his people through his resurrection is stronger than death. However, we will wait until this re-creation for the redemption of our bodies in the resurrection, the last judgment, and the full blessing that comes when God makes all things new. The end of Isaiah takes the long view of salvation, all the way to new heavens and new earth, and so should we.

Another takeaway is the equality of heaven and earth in this new creation. Some groups, such as the Jehovah's Witnesses and other new religious movements, teach that God has a two-tiered reward for believers. A renewed earth will be the home of the good, and heaven for the better. This may seem plausible to some, and we can commend these groups for expecting a new heaven and new earth, but there is no support for this idea of a two-tiered reward in the Old or New Testament. The "new heavens and new earth" are one reality in which God dwells fully, and wherever God's people dwell in them, they are equally blessed.

A final takeaway deals with the punishment of the wicked at the end of time. For many Christians today, this is an uncomfortable topic. All sorts of issues arise when we think about this, and we will address only one of them here. The doctrine of the eternal punishment of the wicked is in fact a biblical teaching. Moreover, it's not a late, afterthought teaching, but it begins here in Isaiah right along with the doctrine of a blessed life in a re-created heaven and earth. Likewise, in Daniel 12:2, where a teaching of the resurrection first appears, it leads to both eternal life and an eternal punishment of "shame and contempt." What is the significance of such a sobering teaching? One of the professors in my doctoral program, Raymond Brown, was a leading New Testament scholar of his generation and a

---

2. Wright, *Surprised by Hope*.

devoted Roman Catholic priest, but in public lectures he often drew questions skeptical of traditional biblical teachings. He was sometimes asked about the doctrine of eternal punishment by Christians who didn't accept it. He typically responded in a simple but thoughtful way: eternal punishment means that God treats evil with an eternal seriousness. I would add this to his point, drawing on Isaiah: it means that God's victory over evil is eternally demonstrated.

QUESTIONS FOR REFLECTION AND DISCUSSION

1. Obituary notices often say that the deceased "went to her/his heavenly home." What might be correct and incorrect about such a statement?
2. What do you think about N. T. Wright's phrase, "Life after life after death"? How might this corrected view of the last things cause us to look at our world differently?
3. Why is it so hard for many Christians today to talk about what the Bible says about the punishment of some at the end of time?
4. Many theologians have said that the Bible's overall vision of the last things is shaped by its vision of the first things: creation and life in the garden of Eden. Do you see any evidence for this observation? What might it mean for you?
5. The comedian and film director Woody Allen once quipped, "The lion and the lamb will lie down together, but the lamb won't get much sleep." Despite the fact that this is a joke, what might it say about how people look at the biblical view of the last things?
6. How does what we believe about the last things inform how we live in the world now?

9

What Plans Does God Have for Us?

For I know the plans I have for you, says the LORD, plans to prosper you and not to harm you, plans to give you hope and a future. (Jeremiah 29:11)

WE NORTH AMERICANS LIVE today in an increasingly nonreligious culture. Social scientists tell us the details about that: declining attendance rates at services, rising numbers of people with no religious affiliation, and the rest—but Christians and followers of other religions know from daily life that it's true. This nonreligious atmosphere impacts the spiritual life of Christians, sometimes in subtle ways. One impact is that many Christians have a declining sense of God's presence in their lives. As a result, Christians are often looking for reassurance that God is present with them, knows them as individuals, and guides their lives for good.

Jeremiah 29:11 seems to offer this reassurance of God's presence and care to Christians today, so it has become one of the most beloved verses of the Bible. Biblegateway.com, a popular website for reading and studying the Bible, has reported that this verse is second only to John 3:16 in the number of times single Bible verses are accessed on its site. Campus Crusade for Christ, a leading evangelical organization now called Cru, drew on this verse at the beginning of its popular *Four Spiritual Laws* pamphlet: "God loves you and has a wonderful plan for your life." Jeremiah 29:11 has probably ended up on more posters, plaques and refrigerator magnets than any other Old Testament verse. It has also found its way into contemporary Christian music (for example, into songs by Bobby Michaels and Martha Munizzi, both titled "I Know the Plans"). In sum, Jeremiah 29:11 is one of the most treasured verses in the Bible today. "I know the plans I have for you, says the Lord, plans to prosper you and not to harm you, plans to give you hope and a future."

This verse sounds like good news for every believer: God has a plan that richly blesses every believer's life. Some people apply this verse to their lives in large ways, to their salvation and their overall relationship with God. Others think that it applies in more everyday ways. They say to others, or perhaps to themselves: "Are you uncertain about what you should do? Don't worry; this verse says that God has a plan for it." Or they say, "Are you having difficulties at work or at home? Hang in there; God is giving you a good future even now." Or this: "Do you have money troubles? There's good news in this verse—God will soon make you prosper." What could be wrong with claiming this verse as our own and applying it to our lives?

As we will see, to apply this verse specifically to our personal situations is to misunderstand it. In fact, its correct explanation is so different from its popular understanding that many Christians today would not want it to apply to them. When Jeremiah 29 opens, the nation of Judah had recently (in 586 B.C.E.) been conquered by the Babylonian Empire, and the city of Jerusalem and its temple were in ruins. Most of its leading citizens and their families—rulers, priests, prophets, local authorities, large landowners, even skilled artisans—were carried off to the land of their conquerors. These exiles probably numbered in the thousands, and they were kept together in one area of the city of Babylon, where they longed for home and freedom. They didn't have a simple case of homesickness, but a crisis of faith expressed in Psalm 137: 4: "How can we sing the Lord's song in a strange land?"

Things were bad in Babylon for the exiles, and just as bad for the people of God left behind in Israel. Physical and spiritual conditions were deplorable. Jeremiah 28, an important part of the context for Jeremiah 29, records a confrontation between the prophet Jeremiah and a false prophet named Hananiah. Hananiah had made a bold promise to the people: God had plans to restore Israel in only two years. The temple would be reestablished, he said, and the exiles would be coming home soon. It sounded good, and Hananiah claimed that it was divinely revealed to him, but in fact it wasn't true. God had no plans to make everything better in two years. God said to Hananiah through Jeremiah, "You have made these people trust in a lie."

In chapter 29, we see similar false hopes play out among the Judean exiles in Babylon. Among the exiles two prophets had arisen who said that they would all return home very soon. The exiles happily believed them, and Jeremiah wrote a letter to the exiles to put an end to these "dreams" (29:8). Despite the predictions of these false prophets, the exiles will be held for a total of seventy years before their exile will end. In the Bible, this is a full life span (Psalm 90:10). Since they had begun their exile only a few years before, the prospect of a seventy-year period of captivity must have been crushing news. Jeremiah advises them to settle in for the long term, marry and give their children in marriage, and "seek the welfare of the city" of Babylon (v. 7, another often misused verse, but we can't treat it here).

Jeremiah has given them the bad news of a long exile, and now it's time for some good news. God promises them that despite this long exile, he has "plans to prosper you and not to harm you, plans to give you hope and a future." But the "you" who will see release is not the people he writes to, but only their descendants, many of them yet unborn. Also, the "you" here is plural, referring to the whole group of Judean exiles, not the singular that could apply to individuals in exile. The Judean exiles can multiply and prosper now in Babylon, but only if they accept their captivity and all its hardships (28:7). This acceptance entails an admission to themselves that they are in a long exile because of their grievous sins against God. They had hoped that their punishment would be short—"Just two more years!" they had said—but it was going to be longer than any of them had imagined. Just as the Israelites had to wander in the wilderness until the whole generation of those who worshiped the golden calf at Mount Sinai was dead, so too the Judeans who had rebelled against God would die in Babylon. Very few of them who understood Jeremiah's letter when it was read to them would live to see their own return; their children might return, and their grandchildren probably would, but they probably would not. Jeremiah promised that God had a plan that was certain and dependable, a plan that would bring "hope and a future," but it would not unfold on Israel's preferred timetable. On the other hand, God's plans for the false prophets gave them no hope and no future. These prophets would be destroyed by the Babylonians. In sum, "I know the plans I have for you to prosper you and not to harm you, plans to give you hope and a future" is for the group as a whole, and the promise of freedom and prosperity is only for the descendants of the Judean exiles. *This* is the "hope" and "future" for the exiles.

Given this verse's significant misinterpretation, do people who fasten on it today get anything right about it? I believe they do. First, they see correctly that God guides human life. This fits what the Bible says overall about the power and providence of God. We may not know *what* God plans for his people, but we know by faith that God does have a plan. This is just as true today as it was in Jeremiah's time. Second, people who misunderstand this verse know that God wants to bless his people to serve him faithfully. Jeremiah's letter calls on them to trust God's plans and obey God's will. Third, most of those who misunderstand this verse know that "hope" and "future" are important terms in the Old Testament, and even more important in the New Testament. God has plans for his people as a whole, and plans for the re-creation of the whole world when Christ comes. This is our hope and our future.

What are the significant takeaways for Christians today who grasp what this verse really means? First, we need to be cautious about claiming as our own any Bible promise we happen to like, especially if we take the promise out of context and give it a meaning it doesn't have. We can't "name it and claim it" and think that God is bound by our claim. God may have other plans for us, as he did for his people in Babylon who named and claimed a quick release. Human plans are not necessarily God's plans. Jeremiah 29:11 is a long ray of hope—not of short-term success and prosperity for each of us as individuals, but of long-term hope for all the people of God. Jeremiah's letter calls on God's people to be faithful here and now, no matter what their circumstances might be. Sometimes this faithfulness means that we must accept diminished expectations for our personal future. We then face the same spiritual issue that the Judean exiles in Babylon faced: When our personal dreams die, and our life changes, can we still serve God trustingly and faithfully?

A second point of significance in Jeremiah 29:11 for today is this. The Bible reveals to us God's overall plan for his people and the whole world, but it does not reveal God's plan for each individual life. Occasionally people who like Jeremiah 29:11 conclude from it, "God has a set plan for my life, and I must find it." The Bible says in different ways that God does know about every individual life, but this verse doesn't say that God reveals this knowledge.[1] We trust in God's guidance for his people even though we don't know the details of where God is leading us in this life as individual believers. God's plans to give us a "hope and a future" are nothing more and nothing less that this: eternal life in Christ for those who trust in him for salvation and follow him, eternal life that begins now and is fully realized when Jesus comes to make all things new.

---

1. Waltke, *Finding the Will of God*, argues cogently that contrary to much popular contemporary evangelical teaching, the Bible does not teach that Christians can find God's special will for their individual lives, and therefore they should not attempt to do so.

This is an ultimate hope and a future, but we humans tend to be inquisitive about our personal futures. People wonder about God's will and plan for their individual life: Where should I go to school? What career should I pursue? Should I get married, and to whom? God's promises are primarily directed to all his people, not to each and every one of us as individuals as we faithfully ponder and puzzle out the direction of our lives. In particular, we must avoid hearing Jeremiah 29:11 in the same way that Jeremiah's contemporaries listened to the false prophet Hananiah, expecting that God will work out everything for our benefit in the very near future and in a way that will please us. We must not confuse our hopes with God's plan.

A third takeaway is this. Almost immediately after this verse, vv. 13–14 state, "You will find me, if you seek me with all your heart ... and I will restore your fortunes and gather you from all the nations and all the places where I have driven you." The restoration of the people of Israel, the main part of God's plans in verse 11, springs from their right relationship with God. The dynamics of relationship with God are the same today. We must seek God, not a happy, easy solution to our perceived needs. Seeking God will not result in fixes for life's problems, or direct knowledge of God's plans for us, as people who misunderstand Jeremiah 29:11 often suppose. Instead, seeking God will help us live within a much bigger story than just our own, one in which God resolves the difficulties and disappointments of life in ways that far exceed our expectations.

QUESTIONS FOR REFLECTION AND DISCUSSION

1. Is this a verse that has had meaning in your own life? If so, how?
2. Why do you think this verse is so popular?
3. Now that you have been exposed to the history behind it, how has your understand of this verse changed?
4. How do you feel about the idea that as Christians we are called to live well into whatever circumstances we find ourselves?
5. Can you think of a time when you may have confused God's plans with your desires? What was the result?
6. What can people do to find out what God is specifically calling them to do with their lives? For instance, what can people do to discern what career to pursue?

10

Should Christians Forgive and Forget?

I will forgive their iniquity, and remember their sin no more. (Jeremiah 31:34)

DOES THE BIBLE TELL us to forgive and forget? Many Christians today would say that this expression comes from the Bible. It has a biblical ring to it, and its similar sounds (*forg*ive and *forg*et) make it easy to remember. Christians use it often and approvingly; forgiving and forgetting seems like a good and godly thing to do. The popular American theologian Lewis Smedes even wrote a book on forgiveness titled *Forgive and Forget*.[1] So ingrained is "forgive and forget" that many Christians doubt whether they have actually forgiven a wrong done to them because they remember when and how it happened, and how hurt they were. As someone once said to me, "If we really forgive others, we will forget the wrongs they did to us."

Despite all this, the Bible does not instruct us to forgive and literally forget. It doesn't address this expectation to us, or even the concept expressed in similar words. Jeremiah 31:34, "I will forgive their iniquity, and remember their sin no more," is the closest the Bible gets to this notion. This verse is quoted in the New Testament, in Hebrews 8:12, which adds to its significance. In another occurrence of "forgive and forget," Isaiah 43:25 says, "I, even I, am he who blots out your transgressions, for my own sake, and remembers your sins no more" (NIV). This verse reappears in Hebrews 10:17: "Their sins and lawless acts I will remember no more" (NIV). The

---

1. Smedes, *Forgive and Forget*.

first thing to notice about these verses is that God is said to forgive and forget; it is not made a command for God's people, at least explicitly. The second thing to notice is that in Hebrew poetry generally, the second line often mirrors the first line in meaning, so "remembering sin no more" can be understood as the equivalent to "forgiving iniquity," not necessarily something in addition to it. Put succinctly, this "forgetting / remembering no more" is poetic, not literal. It emphasizes the completeness of God's forgiveness, not that God loses knowledge of something.

Here is the key verse in its context:

> 31 "The days are coming," declares the LORD, "when I will make a new covenant with the people of Israel and with the people of Judah. 32 It will not be like the covenant I made with their ancestors when I took them by the hand to lead them out of Egypt, because they broke my covenant, though I was a husband to them," declares the LORD. 33 "This is the covenant I will make with the people of Israel after that time," declares the LORD. "I will put my law in their minds and write it on their hearts. I will be their God, and they will be my people. 34 No longer will they teach their neighbor, or say to one another, 'Know the LORD,' because they will all know me, from the least of them to the greatest," declares the LORD. "For I will forgive their wickedness and will remember their sins no more." (NIV)

In this chapter we deal with a large topic, so we must keep our focus on the issue of "forgetting" sin and how it relates to forgiveness. This influential passage from Jeremiah 31 talks powerfully about the "new covenant" God will make with his people. It is often cited as the origin of "forgive and forget" in the Bible. Earlier passages in the Bible exhort the people of God to write God's law on their own minds so they know it, and on their own hearts so they are inclined to do it, but now God will do this directly (v. 33). The covenant idea of "I am your God, you are my people" will be fully realized (v. 33). All of them will have a full knowledge of God, which will come into every member of the people of God (v. 34). The basis of all this (the "For" in v. 34) is God's complete pardon; God will "forgive" their wickedness and "remember their sins no more." "Remember" in the Bible refers to much more than keeping something in one's mind, as it typically does to us. It means to reenact, to keep alive, to keep powerful (compare the words of Holy Communion: "Do this in remembrance of me."). Not remembering sin in Jeremiah 31 means therefore that God will not actively hold our sin against us by punishing us in some way for it. Instead, it will be completely forgiven.

The notion that God literally forgets sin raises a mentally challenging question: Can a God who knows everything—which the Bible clearly affirms and Christians believe—forget anything at all, so that God literally doesn't know it? I believe that many Christians would answer no. God's all-knowing nature is clearly affirmed in several Psalms that are at least as old as the book of Jeremiah. Although God's mind is far beyond our comprehension, we can probably conclude that as far as God has revealed himself to us, nothing is beyond God's knowledge. So when Jeremiah says that God will forget our sins, it means nothing more and nothing less than that our sins will be fully forgiven.

So far we have been discussing "forgive and forget" as it pertains to God, which is how Jeremiah 31 talks of it. Now we turn to an even more complicated topic: Can Christians be expected to literally forget sins done to us, and if so, how? To expect that most Christians will literally forget the wrong that others have done to them is unrealistic. Sometimes that can happen, but it's probably not typical and hardly ever necessary; one can forgive without literally forgetting. This means that we should not doubt whether we have truly forgiven others just because we still remember what they did to us. If we read between the lines of certain New Testament passages, we can see that they imply that Christians are not meant to forget in a literal sense. Take the words of Jesus to Peter to forgive a brother who has sinned repeatedly against him "seventy times seven" times (Matthew 18:22)—if Peter literally "forgave and forgot," he wouldn't be able to number how many times he forgave! In another example, Jesus forgave the woman caught in adultery, but then he said "Go and do not sin [like this] again" (John 8:11). If Jesus literally forgot the woman's sin, how would he know if the woman had done it before if she were brought in front of him again? These examples may seem strained, but they do illustrate that the New Testament's view of forgiveness does not involve literal forgetting.

Forgiveness does not mean ignoring the wrong done to us, or acting as if it didn't happen. If we try to live out "forgive and forget" and come to think that we must forget a wrong done to us after we forgive, then we may find that forgetting is even harder than forgiving. If we "forgive and forget" by saying, "I choose to follow Christ's call to forgive the one who sinned against me, repair our relationship as much as I can, and move on," then we are following God's command to forgive. Every time we pray the Lord's

Prayer we remind ourselves that we must forgive others because God has forgiven us. However, if we decide to "forgive and forget" by saying to ourselves, "I must forgive by acting as if this wrong never occurred, and I will live as if I don't remember it," then we can run into trouble. For example, crime victims can choose to forgive the people who have harmed them, but this does not mean they should act as if the crime and the sin never happened to them.

Psychologists have researched interpersonal forgiveness in depth, and we should summarize their conclusions here and relate them to Christian teaching. Forgiveness is typically defined in psychology as a process that involves a change in emotion and attitude regarding an offender. Most view this as beginning with a deliberate decision to forgive that starts an intentional and voluntary process. Forgiveness results in decreased motivation to retaliate or maintain estrangement from an offender despite their actions, and requires letting go negative emotions toward an offender. Scientific experiments on forgiveness show that it leads to an improved emotional state, lowers the rate of emotional troubles such as anxiety and depression, and even lowers blood pressure. In general, forgiveness improves physical well-being and leads to a greater sense of self-control.[2] It's not hard to see how this relates closely to Christian ideas of forgiveness. In Christianity, forgiveness begins with a decision, typically when God's command to forgive those who sin against us is heard in our conscience. It is a process that requires a letting go, which is the root meaning of the Greek word for "forgiveness." Christian forgiveness entails not only changing our attitudes toward those who have harmed us but also renewing relationships with those who have sinned against us. Renewing these relationships may be even more difficult than changing our attitudes. However, to use the apostle Paul's positive but realistic wording, "If it is possible, so far as it depends on you, live peaceably with all" (Romans 12:18). To this we are called.

What is the significance of all this for us today? First, it means that forgiveness is a process, not a one-time, instant event. Coming to a decision to forgive is not likely right after a bitter experience—for example, a tragic divorce or an unjust job loss. As soon as we can, we should decide to forgive. It might take some time to wrestle with, and pray over, our own feelings before we can start to forgive.

Second, since forgiveness does not entail a literal forgetting; it's normal for memories of past wrongs done to us to be triggered by new wrongs.

---

2. American Psychological Association, *Forgiveness*, 5–6.

When thoughts of past hurts occur, it does not mean that our forgiveness is incomplete. As Lewis Smedes wrote, "You do not have to forget after you forgive; you may, but your forgiving can be sincere even if you remember."[3]

Third, the basis of our forgiving others should never be forgotten: God in Christ has forgiven us. Forgiveness can be studied psychologically, but it's more than a psychological thing. It does us emotional and even physical good, but Scripture never points to this as a motivation for forgiving. Good happens as a by-product; forgiveness is mainly done for Christ's sake, not ours. In other words, forgiveness is primarily a "vertical" thing in which we deal first and foremost with God, not primarily a "horizontal" thing in which dealing with others is foremost. The physical shape of the Latin cross used most frequently as the symbol of Christianity, with a longer vertical beam and a shorter horizontal beam, reminds us of the "vertical" relationship we have with God and the "horizontal" relationship we have with other humans. Our relationship with God, built on what God does for us in grace, is the larger thing, like the vertical beam of the Latin cross. This grace flows from the top down on this vertical beam: from God to us. The "horizontal" relationship, with other people, depends on our relationship with God, just as the horizontal beam of the cross is tied or nailed to the vertical beam. Both the "vertical" and "horizontal" are needed to have an effective Christian life, especially to follow Jesus in forgiving others.

QUESTIONS FOR REFLECTION AND DISCUSSION

1. What did "forgive and forget" mean to you before you read this chapter?
2. Given all the personal benefits of forgiving others, why isn't it easier and done more often? In other words, what prevents us from forgiving? Or, why is forgiveness so difficult?
3. Should the fact that forgiveness is beneficial to us be a reason for forgiving others?
4. In the Lord's Prayer we are reminded to forgive the sins of others, and this is connected to how God has forgiven us. Do we earn God's forgiveness by forgiving others? Why or why not?

---

3. Smedes, *Forgive and Forget*, 49.

5. Do you think that the decision to forgive others is the most important, or the most difficult, part of the whole process of forgiveness? Why, or why not?

6. What is your own understanding of the "vertical" and "horizontal" aspects of the Christian life? How do these relationships play out in your own life?

11

Was Jesus Born in a Manger?

And she gave birth to her firstborn son and wrapped him in bands of cloth, and laid him in a manger, because there was no place for them in the inn. (Luke 2:7)

PARENTS HAVE OCCASIONALLY SCOLDED their children after some instance of bad behavior by saying, "Were you born in a barn?" This expression is not heard so much today, perhaps because barns aren't as common as they used to be. Jesus may have been born in a literal barn, or as we will see below, in a shelter for animals, attached to a house. But every year at Christmas time we hear something different, about Jesus being "born in a manger." For example, the popular song "You are the Living Word" by the contemporary singer Fred Hammond says, "Jesus, Jesus, that's what we call you; / manger born, but on a tree / you died to save humanity." Mariah Carey's Christmas-album song "Jesus, Oh What a Wonderful Child" features the phrase "Born in a lowly manger." The first line of a traditional hymn from 1927, "Redeemer Divine" by Elsie Duncan Yale, is "Born in a manger so lowly." You might hear people use "born in a manger," or see it on Christmas cards.

Was Jesus actually born in a manger? To find the answer, let's take a close look at this verse. It summarizes three events in quick succession. First, Mary "gave birth to her firstborn son." Next, she "wrapped him in bands of cloth." Older translations call these "swaddling cloths," and it's a common mistake today to call them swaddling clothes. These bands of cloth were wrapped tightly around a baby from the neck all the way down.

The tight-fitting cloths provided not just physical support but also emotional security for newborns. Finally, Mary "laid him in a manger, because there was no room for them in the inn." Jesus' placement in a manger is mentioned last, after birth and after wrapping. Being placed in a manger is unusual for the time, and has no direct connection with Old Testament passages that early Christians looked on as prophesying the coming of Jesus. Centuries of pious Christian imagination have made the manger ordinary, but the fact that Luke has to explain why the baby Jesus was laid in a manger—"because there was no place for them in the inn"—indicates it wasn't common at all. Also, that the baby will be "lying in a manger" is a "sign" for the shepherds in Luke 2:12 confirms that a manger is an unusual place to find a newborn baby.

It's clear that to say "Jesus was born in a manger" is to misunderstand Luke 2:7. A manger is a feed trough, more often in the Middle East carved of stone than made of wood, because stone is impervious to moisture. Mangers were situated in animal stalls, stalls that were often on the ground level of the animal owner's house or in a cave near the house. (Even today some European farmhouses are connected to animal stalls.) The Greek word for "manger" is used this way most famously in the ancient fable by the Greek moralist Aesop, "The Dog in the Manger." This dog lies in a manger and barks at the animals that come to feed from it, but of course he doesn't eat the straw himself. The story points out the foolishness of persons who withhold from others something useless to themselves.

A slight complication crops up here that muddies the issue of where Jesus was born, and may have contributed to the misunderstanding. Although the Greek word for "manger" most often means "feed trough," it can also mean (with much less frequency) a "stall" for feeding or sheltering animals. It usually does not refer to a separate building like a barn or a feeding shed. People who think that "Jesus was born in a manger" could be thinking that the manger is a stall, because a stall is often pictured in art about Jesus' birth and on Christmas cards. However, here in Luke 2:7 the context lets us understand clearly which one of these meanings Luke intends. "Manger" fits "feed trough" in Luke 2, not "stall," because it doesn't make much sense to say "She laid him in an animal stall" if Jesus had been born in an animal stall. Luke is much too careful a writer to say such a clumsy thing.

The notion that Jesus was literally born in a feed trough is both doubtful and nonsensical. It never would have occurred to a woman to give birth while situated in a feed trough, which is what "born in a manger" literally—and ludicrously—means. Childbirth is painful enough without that sort of awkward positioning! We don't have any detailed description of childbirth in the Bible, which should not surprise us, given that in Semitic culture such intimate events were not spoken of openly, much less written down in detail. The general description of childbirth we have says that women gave birth while kneeling, squatting or sitting, so that gravity would help with the process. The Bible also says that children may be born "on the knees of" another person (Genesis 50:23; see also Job 3:12). This implies that childbirth took place while the mother was sitting on the knees of a woman who was helping her, facing this woman and leaning on her for physical and emotional support. Special furniture may have been used as well. Exodus 1:16 speaks of "birthing stools." The Romans had a special birthing chair with a U-shaped seat and special supports for the back and feet, and it is possible that this was used in Jewish culture of Jesus' time as well. If you are wondering how Mary knew about childbirth, it was common at this time for young girls to be present when relatives were giving birth, in part to familiarize them with the process. Also, a midwife likely helped with Jesus' birth, since husbands generally didn't have the foggiest notion of what to do, and were expected to stay away! At any rate, according to the Gospel of Luke, Mary herself laid Jesus in a manger after he was born "because there was no place for them in the inn" (2:7). This manger would have made a safe, secure place in which to lay the baby Jesus, and both mother and baby could rest.

What are the takeaways from the correction of this misunderstanding? First, even though Jesus was not "born in a manger," he was laid in a manger as a symbol of humility. (Those who misunderstand this verse as "born in a manger" are correct in understanding it as a sign of humbleness.) Being laid in a manger is a humble way for the Son of God to rest after his birth. Later Christian tradition romanticizes this by suggesting that Jesus welcomed the animals and received their attention. This is a pleasant thought, and it probably developed from the idea that some animals may have been puzzled by a baby in their feed trough. It lines up with the Christian belief that Jesus came (and is coming again) to bring peace to the whole creation. However, it's probably not what Luke means here. He is focused on the humility of Jesus at his birth, and humility will be a leading theme of Luke's entire gospel. The same Jesus who had such a humble bed as a newborn in Luke 2 said later in Luke, "Foxes have holes, and birds their nests, but the Son of Man has nowhere to lay his head" (9:58). Symmetry shapes the beginning and end of Jesus' life. At his birth he was wrapped in cloth, and laid in a borrowed manger. When he died, he was wrapped in cloth and laid in a borrowed tomb.

Here is a second takeaway from this chapter: Luke and Matthew tell the story of Jesus' conception at some length, but tell of his birth quickly, with fewer details. Why? Several reasons could be given, but perhaps they want readers to focus on the basics. Jesus was conceived within Mary in an unusual, miraculous way but had a normal human birth. Because the New Testament gives relatively little attention to the birth of Jesus—the Gospels of Mark and John don't narrate it at all—curious readers of every age have wondered about its details. Beginning in the second century, "infancy gospels" were written to provide these details, some quite popular. Christians from the second century until today have added to Matthew 1–2 and Luke 1–2, and it has shaped the way that people understand this story.

Here is a way that many people today, Bible readers or not, frame what I call the common Christmas story: "About two thousand years ago, on the snowy evening of December 25, Mary rode into Bethlehem on a donkey led by Joseph. They urgently searched for a place for Mary to deliver her baby. The innkeeper could put them up only in a barn in back of the inn. Mary gave birth to Jesus in a manger, and dressed him in swaddling clothes. That same night, angels sang to shepherds near Bethlehem, and the shepherds went to Bethlehem with some of their sheep. There they joined three kings, who had just arrived on their camels, in worshiping the completely quiet newborn."

The elements of this story are repeated often in art and song, but not a single sentence of it agrees with the New Testament. Jesus was probably not born "in the bleak midwinter," as a Christmas carol says, because sheep are not kept in the open fields during winter, when the grass is not suitable for grazing. No donkey for Mary's travel is mentioned by Luke or Matthew. Luke's statement "while she was there" can imply an indefinite stay in Bethlehem before Jesus was born; Luke's phrase certainly does not imply that Mary was about to go into labor as she arrived in Bethlehem. (The beautiful Mexican ritual *las posadas*—"the lodgings"—acts out this pressured search for housing.) The animal stall where Jesus was likely born was probably not a separate barn, as we have discussed above, but part of a house. Jesus was not "born in a manger," but laid in a manger after his birth. Swaddling is done with strips of cloth, not clothes. Angels appeared to the shepherds, but Luke does not say that they sang to them; he uses the ordinary word "said." Angels speak to humans, but they sing only to God, and only in praise. It wasn't likely that the shepherds brought any sheep with them to Bethlehem, and Luke doesn't mention it. Sheep are depicted in art to identify the visitors as shepherds. Matthew mentions "wise men from the East," but doesn't say that there are three of them. That there are three is deduced probably from the three gifts listed (gold, frankincense, and myrrh), and Matthew implies that the wise men arrived much later than on the day Jesus was born. Finally, the notion that baby Jesus was wonderfully quiet (for example, in "The little Lord Jesus, no crying he makes," from the Christmas hymn "Away in a Manger") is perhaps too pious. Babies cry at times, in particular at birth, and Jesus was no exception.

Despite all these misconceptions that got attached to the story of Jesus' birth like barnacles to a sleek ship's hull, what Luke and Matthew actually say about Jesus—his conception, birth and afterward—is much more marvelous than these additions. We should fix our attention on the main things that the gospels *do* say. Jesus was conceived in the Virgin Mary by divine action. He was born in a humble way, and the story of his birth hints at the gospel story that it introduces. In all of this he will "save his people from their sins," and in fulfilling the messianic hopes of Israel, Jesus brings salvation to the whole world. Why should this amazing story need any embellishment?

A third takeaway from a correction of the misunderstanding that "Jesus was born in a manger" is this brief suggestion: Let's quote the Bible carefully even when it doesn't make a big difference. Saying that Jesus was "born in a manger" does not result in a doctrinal mistake or do significant harm to the Christian life, but that's not the point. What the Bible actually says is important, so we should pay attention to the details. If we are careful to quote the little things correctly, we will become more careful in quoting and applying the big things. Let's be careful to say that Jesus was "laid in a manger," not that he was "born in a manger."

QUESTIONS FOR REFLECTION AND DISCUSSION

1. Until you read this study, what was your understanding of the manger?
2. Have you ever said that Jesus was "born in a manger"? If so, what did you mean by it? What do you think is significant about Jesus being connected with a manger?
3. Did you assume that any other parts of what I call the common Christmas story were actually part of the biblical story? If so, which ones?
4. Beside the "laid in a manger" statement, what other indications of humility are found in Luke's story of Jesus' birth?
5. Some people argue that the conception and birth of Jesus should not be that important for Christians today given the fact that Mark and John don't narrate it at all. What do you think of such an argument?
6. Do you think that the things that have grown up around the biblical account of Jesus' birth in the way we celebrate Christmas help or hinder Christian life today? Why?

12

Don't Judge at All?

Judge not, that you be not judged. (Matthew 7:1)

ONE OF THE MOST frequently heard expressions today is, "I'm not judging." This is often said by someone who has just said something negative about others but doesn't want to be thought less of for saying it. Many Christians and even some who are not Christians invoke the Bible verse "Judge not, that you be not judged," as the basis of this attitude. They say, referring to Matthew 7:1, "Jesus said that you shouldn't judge!" Using this verse is a favorite way for many people to accuse Christians of being judgmental and hypocritical. The intriguing book *Unchristian: What a New Generation Really Thinks about Christianity . . . and Why it Matters*[1] found that almost 90 percent of non-Christians in their twenties call Christians "judgmental." This was the strongest complaint against Christians from this group. Most of them also view Christians as "hypocrites."

The related expression "Who am I to judge?" is now used by ordinary people and leaders of society. Even Pope Francis used it in 2013 about gay priests, and a good deal of public discussion ensued. We hear "Who am I to judge?" in television and films, and in everyday life. For example, someone may say, "Yes, he stole from the clients he worked for, but who am I to judge? We're all sinners, after all! 'Judge not'—that's what Jesus said." When used in this way, "Judge not" forbids declaring any specific action wrong,

---

1. Kinnamon and Lyons, *Unchristian*.

since that would mean judging someone. In the ethos of our times, where tolerance is a supreme cultural value, this idea that judging others is wrong is a widespread notion. Judging is thought to contribute to hateful talk, even to bullying and violence, so there is a big push toward a judgment-free society. For example, the Planet Fitness chain of health clubs began a "Judgment-Free Generation" initiative in 2016 that seeks to promote tolerance and acceptance across America. (That this chain also claims that its gyms are "Judgment Free Zones," places where people who need to exercise are not disrespected, is not incidental, of course!) The most extreme use of "Don't judge" that I have heard was spoken by a college professor who said about the Holocaust, "We shouldn't judge the Germans who did this, because we can't know what they were going through." This comment sparked anger, and rightly so, but the remark does raise the question of whether there is a limit to being nonjudgmental.

Was Jesus really saying that his followers should not judge anybody else for any reason? It certainly seems that way if we look at this verse only by itself. Or is he saying something else, something that fastening on this verse without understanding its context doesn't capture? Something else is indeed being said: the problem is hypocrisy, not judging itself. We start by reading Matthew 7:1–6.

> 1 Do not judge, or you too will be judged. ² For in the same way you judge others, you will be judged, and with the measure you use, it will be measured to you. ³ Why do you look at the speck of sawdust in your brother's eye and pay no attention to the plank in your own eye? ⁴ How can you say to your brother, 'Let me take the speck out of your eye,' when all the time there is a plank in your own eye? ⁵ You hypocrite, first take the plank out of your own eye, and then you will see clearly to remove the speck from your brother's eye. ⁶ Do not give dogs what is sacred; do not throw your pearls to pigs. If you do, they may trample them under their feet, and turn and tear you to pieces. (NIV)

Despite how it appears if one takes this verse out of its context and makes it an independent rule, this passage in Matthew is not forbidding judgment. The problem is not good judgment that is honest with ourselves and helpful to others; rather, the problem is hypocrisy that taints our judgment. A close reading of this passage shows this. By itself, and taken literally, "Do not judge, or you too will be judged" could mean that one may escape God's judgment at the end of time by not judging the behavior of others. However, this would contradict the Bible's consistent teaching that everyone is judged by God at the end of time. In v. 2, Jesus goes on to state "Judge not" in a positive way: "For in the same way you judge others, you will be judged [by God], and with the measure you use, it will be measured to you [by God]." (I have inserted "by God" to make it clear that divine action, not human action, is implied. This verse does *not* mean that if we don't judge others, others won't judge us.) Jesus expects that his followers will judge others, but warns that they will be judged in a like manner.

In vv. 3–4 the warning against hypocrisy becomes explicit: "Why do you look at the speck of sawdust in your brother's eye and pay no attention to the plank in your own eye? How can you say to your brother, 'Let me take the speck out of your eye,' when all the time there is a plank in your own eye?" Jesus' audience would have chuckled at this thought of a plank of wood being lodged in someone's eye, a classic example of overstatement. This may be an example of what we call comic relief in otherwise challenging teaching. The NIV brings out something important in the Greek original that is not clear enough in many English translations: the "speck" and "plank/log" are of the same material: here, wood. This makes the hypocrisy more obvious and blatant, because the same kind of sin we see in others is much bigger in ourselves. This hypocrisy makes judgment ineffective; it's hard to see a grain of sawdust in someone else's eye when we have an unnoticed plank of lumber in ours! In this circumstance, judgment is rejected by the person who receives it, and it corrupts the person who offers it. Jesus then explains in v. 5 how to judge rightly, but first he makes it obvious what is going on in judgment like this: "You hypocrite." This is a sharp thing to say—some might even call it judgmental—but it shows what Jesus is really concerned about here. "First take the plank out of your own eye, and then you will see clearly to remove the speck from your brother's eye." The command "take the speck out of your brother's eye" certainly gives permission to judge so long as we judge rightly.

There are two possible responses to Jesus' command not to judge until we first deal with our own problems. The first assumes that no one can live up to Jesus' standards, even in a basic way, and so no one should ever judge anyone else, since "we're all sinners." This is a popular option in today's culture, which, as we said above, emphasizes tolerance and being nonjudgmental as important social values. This rejection of judgment can be seen in a trenchant statement by the theologian H. Richard Niebuhr, who decades ago offered a negative summary of the theology of many mainline

American Protestant churches as, "A God without wrath brought men without sin into a Kingdom without judgment through the ministrations of a Christ without a Cross."[2]

The second possibility is that we should all amend our own lives and live properly before helping others to do the same. This second option, it's clear in the whole passage, is what Jesus intends. Jesus commands us to withhold judgment, not only judgment in our thoughts but especially judgment spoken to someone else, until we change our own life. Jesus as presented in Matthew actually expects that his followers can do this—not perfectly, but well enough. Jesus' point is that only after correcting one's own behavior will one see clearly enough to make adequate judgments and help others correct their behavior. This recognizes the human tendency to judge based on seeing ourselves in others. If we are greedy, we tend to see a lot of greed in other people. If we are arrogant, we tend to suspect arrogance in many others. If we are lustful, we tend to suspect sexual desires and misconduct in others. As long as we don't deal with our faults, we will have a tendency to see them in everyone else. Most of this is explained by psychologists as an unwitting self-image defense tactic. We can use it to deny that we have any problem, or to say, "I may have a problem with such-and-such a behavior, but that person has a much bigger one with it, so I'm not so bad after all."

The last verse of this passage may seem at first glance to be unrelated to the topic of judging, but it is exactly on topic. When Jesus says, "Do not give dogs what is sacred; do not throw your pearls to pigs," he requires good judgment. Jesus is not talking about literal dogs and pigs here; he is speaking about people who do not live in God's way. Not giving what is holy or precious to people who reject God requires judging who the "dogs" and "pigs" are.

What do people who misunderstand this verse get right about it? Sometimes when people complain about others being judgmental, they mean that they are always judging and criticizing. Where this is true, it is a legitimate complaint. Anyone who is constantly criticizing others is certainly disobeying Jesus' commands and will not be effective in changing attitudes and behaviors in others. Also, people who are judged can often see hypocrisy in those who judge them.

This challenging passage has three main implications for Christian life today. First, no Christian is perfect. If Jesus had expected literal perfection

---

2. Niebuhr, *Kingdom of God in America*, 193.

from us, he would not have taught us to pray every day "Forgive us our sins." (This means that "Be perfect as your Father in heaven is perfect" in Matthew 5:48 should be taken in the sense of "be mature," not "be sinless.") Not even the most mature, dedicated Christian is going to be completely self-aware and nonhypocritical—in other words, a perfect evaluator of human behavior. Because we make judgments as flawed people, we need to take special care in doing so with honesty and humility. But each one of us does have a responsibility to deal with our own faults, and then help other Christians remedy their own. Throughout his ministry Jesus emphasized repentance, faith in God, and obedience to God. Once these things are active in us, although our thoughts and actions will never be perfect in this world, good judgment can and must be made. The church in particular cannot exist faithfully and well without some basic level of good judgment by leaders and laity alike.

Second, it may be helpful to think about how these principles work in the practice of one element of the Christian life, forgiveness. Forgiveness of others assumes a judgment: we know that someone has done us wrong. This wrong is real, not just a misunderstanding on our part, and is not affected by our own level of hypocrisy. The wrong is overcome in us by the extension of mercy toward the offender, in our own mind and then as fully as possible in relationship. Jesus requires that people forgive one another as God has forgiven us. Again, Jesus' command both assumes judgment and encourages a merciful response.

Finally, one caution is important. The New Testament speaks primarily about judgment within the Christian community, not Christian judgment of individuals outside it. In our passage from Matthew 7, Jesus speaks of judgment on the "brother and sister," that is, on a follower of Christ. Identifying the "wolf in sheep's clothing"—those who are "known by their fruits" in Matthew 7:15–20 is also a reference to other believers, in particular to "false prophets." The apostle Paul called for decisive judgment of other Christians, but then he added, "What have I to do with judging outsiders? Is it not those inside the church whom you are to judge? God judges those outside" (1 Corinthians 5:12–13). As a part of their witness to the gospel, Christians should make God's expectations for human life widely known, and call all people to repentance and faith. But passing judgment on individuals outside the faith is unbiblical and unnecessary.

QUESTIONS FOR REFLECTION AND DISCUSSION

1. How does knowing that the "speck" and the "plank" are the same sort of wrong affect your understanding of this verse? Was this a new insight for you?

2. Does Jesus' talk of "pigs" and "dogs" at the end of this passage seem harsh to you? Why might Jesus talk this way?

3. As a spiritual exercise, keep track for one whole day of how you think and speak critically of others. Reflect on any patterns you might see in it. Is this the plank in your eye?

4. One website on the Sermon on the Mount titles its treatment of this section, "How to Be Judgmental in God's Way." What might be helpful and unhelpful about this title?

5. What do you think is involved in "first tak[ing] the plank from your own eye"?

6. Is it fair that people outside the church often see those inside it as hypocrites? How should Christians react to such complaints?

13

If We Ask, Will We Really Receive?

Ask, and it will be given to you; seek, and you will find; knock, and the door will be opened for you. (Matthew 7:7)

THE PEOPLE OF GOD are used to asking God in prayer for many things. The book of Psalms is filled with petitions by the psalmists for themselves and for others. Jesus himself taught us to ask daily for one necessity of life: "Give us this day our daily bread." He also taught us to ask for God's forgiveness for our sins. Most of these requests in prayer are quite routine, and that's as it should be. But at times in almost every Christian's life, we ask God for particular things with deep fervor. Christians ask to be delivered from disease, to find a good spouse, to have children, to find emotional peace, to be rid of a difficult temptation or burden, and more.

Matthew 7:7, "Ask and you will receive," is correctly understood to encourage our expectant prayers, but it is also misconstrued. The common misunderstanding of this verse comes in two parts. The first is an expectation that God will always answer our prayers the way we like. "Ask, and it will be given to you; seek, and you will find; knock, and the door will be opened for you" seems plain to most Christians who read it. It also seems very promising—all you have to do is ask, seek, or knock, and God will give you what you are looking for. Jesus doesn't seem to specify how long or how intently we have to ask. Some Christian experience would seem to support this misunderstanding, because at times we do receive quickly what we ask for. This happens, for example, when one undergoes medical testing for cancer or some other dreaded disease, prays fervently while tissue samples are tested, and in a few days receives the "all clear" notice from the doctor. But when believers pray for something and don't receive it in a timely way, or if God's answer seems to be no, which in everyday Christian life happens just as often, they may wonder if they did something wrong in their prayers or in their life. The second part of the misunderstanding is to think that "ask" means "ask for anything." Matthew 7:7 doesn't seem to put any limits on what we can ask, seek, and knock for; instead, it seems to invite all sorts of prayers for all sorts of things, and many Christians have used this verse that way. But as we will see, this is a self-serving misunderstanding of what Jesus tells us.

To get at the real meaning of this famous verse, let's look at it in Matthew 7 now. After teaching about judgment and hypocrisy in 7:1–6, Jesus begins a new, unrelated topic:

> 7 Ask and it will be given to you; seek and you will find; knock and the door will be opened to you. 8 For everyone who asks receives; the one who seeks finds; and to the one who knocks, the door will be opened. 9 Which of you, if your son asks for bread, will give him a stone? 10 Or if he asks for a fish, will give him a snake? 11 If you, then, though you are evil, know how to give good gifts to your children, how much more will your Father in heaven give good gifts to those who ask him! (NIV)

A few things are important to notice in v. 7. First, the form of the imperatives in Greek implies continual action in prayer, which can be paraphrased like this: "ask, and keep on asking"; "seek, and keep seeking"; "knock, and keep on knocking." Second, the threefold command, "ask, seek, knock," indicates a fullness of petition. All three words have a rich background in the Bible, where asking God to grant prayer requests is common, seeking things is commended in many of Jesus' parables, and knocking on closed doors is expected, even invited. In particular, the use of "seek" and "find" would call to mind, for members of Jesus' audience who knew their Bible well, Jeremiah 29:13–14: "When you seek me, you will find me; if you seek me with all your heart, I will let you find me, says the LORD." Third, the passive verbs in this verse, "be given" and "be opened," indicate divine action. It was common for some Jews at this time to avoid saying the name of God too often, so they used the passive voice. "Ask, and it will be given" means "ask, and God will give it to you"; "knock, and it will be opened" was heard as "knock, and God will open the door."

The message of v. 7 is stated again in v. 8. This repetition makes God's promise to answer prayer even more certain, and the language of v. 8 is more emphatic as well. "*Everyone* who asks receives"; in the structure of the Greek used here, the "everyone" also extends by implication to "the one who seeks" and "the one who knocks." They effectively become "everyone who seeks" and "everyone who knocks." In vv. 9–10, Jesus gives the rationale behind this promise, that God is disposed to give us good things, but at first the wording may seem strange to us: "Which of you, if your son asks for bread, will give him a stone? Or if he asks for a fish, will give him a snake?" We might ask, why would anyone give a stone for bread, or a snake for fish? This probably relates to the overall shape of a small loaf of bread and a medium-sized stone, which would have much the same size and shape. Similarly, fish from the Sea of Galilee in Jesus' day were typically long and thin, and could resemble the shape of a snake.

In verse 11, Jesus seems to make a harsh judgment about his hearers: "You are evil." But he adds immediately, "you know how to give good things to your children." Why this negative comment? Jesus' teaching reflects that we belong to a fallen world and participate both intentionally and unintentionally in this fallenness, so we are in fact evil. However, this obviously doesn't mean that we are as evil as we can be, just that evil has warped the image of God within us. Here Jesus uses an interpretive technique called "light to heavy": if something is true for a small thing, it is just as true, and more important, for a big thing. If human parents in their lives compromised by evil normally know how to give good things to their children, God, who is completely good and gracious, will "much more" give good things to those who pray for them. This should be an assurance to those whom Jesus has called evil; an added assurance is implied in this verse: that we are God's children.

Now we can apply this treatment of the passage to misunderstandings of v. 7. "Ask and you will receive" builds on an important theme in Jesus' teaching on prayer: the theme of faithful persistence. We are to persist in prayer, even when we keep on asking and still don't receive. We must keep praying even if we think God isn't listening, or isn't answering to our liking. This strengthens our faith, and makes us better Christians than if all our prayers were answered quickly and happily. If we received from God whatever we asked soon after we asked for it—with the instant gratification we North Americans often expect these days—we would not have to be persistent in prayer, and we would not be prayerful people. Our faith would then be shallow and hollow. Jesus teaches us here to pray expectantly, to pray constantly, and to pray faithfully, but we must not think that we obligate God to grant our request if we do so.

The parallel passage in Luke 11 sheds a good deal of light on "Ask, seek, knock" in Matthew 7:7 and confirms the correct understanding of this saying. "Ask, seek, knock" in Luke 11:9 is part of a larger narrative in which we are told what to ask, seek and knock for. After Jesus has defended Mary against her sister, Martha, for seeking what matters most (Luke 10:38–42), being an attentive disciple of Jesus, Jesus' followers ask their teacher how to pray (11:1). Jesus teaches them in his special prayer for his followers to ask for several things: the hallowing (praising) of God's name, the coming of God's kingdom rule, daily bread, the forgiveness of their sins, and deliverance from severe trial (11:2–4). Jesus then commands persistence in a short parable (11:5–8), and then draws an application from this parable, "So I say to you, Ask and it will be given to you" (11:9–13). Luke's context of "Ask and it will be given you" makes it clear that Jesus is not saying "Ask for anything you want, and you will get it." Rather, he says, "Ask for the things of my kingdom, and you will have them." This is made even more certain by the important conclusion that Luke gives to this section when he reports Jesus saying, "How much more will the heavenly Father give the Holy Spirit to those who ask him!" (v. 13). All the "things" that God wants to give us are contained in gift of the Holy Spirit. This effectively rules out self-seeking prayers for money, power, easy happiness, and other benefits that have little or nothing to do with the Holy Spirit.

What parts of the misunderstanding of Matthew 7:7 might be correct? Three significant aspects of the misunderstanding do get "Ask and you will receive" right. First, it correctly understands that Jesus commands us to pray. Christianity, like Judaism, emphasizes the importance of daily prayer, and a part of this is our personal petitions. Second, we are allowed, even encouraged, to pray for our own needs, with the proviso that we will pray more widely as well. Third, we must pray expectantly. God wants us to pray, and God wants to grant our requests.

What are the takeaways for a corrected understanding of this verse? First, asking expectantly and faithfully means asking continuously. We are to persist in prayer, to "keep on keeping on" in it, even if it seems that God is not answering our prayer. We do this not to wear God down with our requests but to show God and ourselves that we are faithful to his command to pray this way. Continuous, faithful prayer forms us into the kind of children that God expects us to be. When praying like this gets difficult, a line from George Croly's hymn, "Spirit of God, Descend Upon My Heart," can be especially meaningful: "Teach me the patience of unanswered prayer."

Second, we should learn to ask for the big things of God's kingdom before we ask God for personal requests. To pray this way reminds us that we are a part of a much larger story than our own life, and puts our own requests in a fuller, better context. The Lord's Prayer, which Jesus gave in part as a model for all our prayers, teaches us to ask first for God's name to be hallowed (praised) and for God's kingdom to come, which will bring God's will to earth. Only then are requests to be made for ourselves: for daily bread, for forgiveness, for protection against evil.

Third, when God grants our prayer, we should make our thanksgiving as ardent as our asking was. It's relatively easy to be fervent in prayer when we are in deep need of God's gifts, but when God grants them, how fervent is our thanksgiving? For example, if we are delivered from disease, is a simple "Thank you" preceded by a "Whew!" enough, and then we become forgetful of God's blessing? A single "thank you" may be good between people in social situations, but because of God's grace, "a song of praise is seemly" (Psalm 147:1, RSV), and this song should be sung many times.

QUESTIONS FOR REFLECTION AND DISCUSSION

1. "Ask" in "Ask and you will receive" has a settled meaning for most Christians, as requests in prayer. What might be the wider meanings of "seek/search" and "knock" in the way we live?

2. Might the practice of avoiding saying God's name so often be a good one for us today? Why? Is there a wise balance to be found here?

3. One verse often quoted in connection with Matthew 7:7 is James 4:3, "You do not have, because you do not ask. You ask and do not receive, because you ask wrongly, in order to spend what you get on your pleasures." What light might this verse shed on the understanding of "Ask and you will receive" in Matthew and Luke?

4. In 2 Corinthians 12:7b–10, Paul relates that he asked God to remove a "thorn in the flesh," but God said no, because "my grace is sufficient

for you." (See chapter 22, below.) What does this answer of no from God mean for understanding "Ask and you will receive"?

5. How can we learn "the patience of unanswered prayer"?

6. What has been your own experience in expectant, long-term prayer?

14

Who Are "the Least of These"?

Truly I tell you, just as you did it to one of the least of these brothers and sisters of mine, you did it to me. (Matthew 25:40)

MOST CHRISTIANS WOULD AGREE that caring for the poor is an important part of the Christian life, a command clearly found in both the Old Testament and the New Testament. Matthew 25:40 is often said to emphasize this duty dramatically and powerfully. At the last judgment, Jesus the judge commends those who care for "the least of these" and condemns those who don't, and in this is an implicit but strong command to care for those in need. Many, perhaps most Christians today think that "the least of these" refers to all the poor and marginalized in the world.

Doubtless the most influential person of our time to hold this view was Mother Teresa, the Roman Catholic nun, now declared a saint, who had a special ministry to the sick and dying of India. When asked to describe the essence of the Christian message, Teresa would often hold up a child's hand and recite Matthew 25:40: "Just as you did it to one of the least of these my brothers, you did it to me." She would then hold the child's fingers one by one and repeat these five words one by one: "You ... did ... it ... to ... me." Mother Teresa saw Jesus in every needy person to whom she ministered, and understood "the least of these" as the poor and distressed.

But is Jesus really talking about the poor and distressed in general here? That might seem to some like a meaningless argument over words, but Jesus ties the eternal destiny of all people to how they treat "the least of these my brothers and sisters." It's not an easy question to deal with because there is a large mismatch in modern times between the current popular understanding of this verse on the one hand and what both a strong majority of biblical scholars and the tradition of the church have understood about it on the other. As we will see, it is a misunderstanding to think that "the least of these" refers to all poor, sick, or otherwise marginalized people.

First, let's read the whole passage carefully. Jesus says,

> 31 When the Son of Man comes in his glory, and all the angels with him, he will sit on the throne of his glory. 32 All the nations will be gathered before him, and he will separate people one from another as a shepherd separates the sheep from the goats, 33 and he will put the sheep at his right hand and the goats at the left.
>
> 34 Then the king will say to those at his right hand, "Come, you that are blessed by my Father, inherit the kingdom prepared for you from the foundation of the world; 35 for I was hungry and you gave me food, I was thirsty and you gave me something to drink, I was a stranger and you welcomed me, 36 I was naked and you gave me clothing, I was sick and you took care of me, I was in prison and you visited me."
>
> 37 Then the righteous will answer him, "Lord, when was it that we saw you hungry and gave you food, or thirsty and gave you something to drink? 38 And when was it that we saw you a stranger and welcomed you, or naked and gave you clothing? 39 And when was it that we saw you sick or in prison and visited you?" 40 And the king will answer them, "Truly I tell you, just as you did it to one of the least of these my brothers and sisters, you did it to me."
>
> 41 Then he will say to those at his left hand, "You that are accursed, depart from me into the eternal fire prepared for the devil and his angels; 42 for I was hungry and you gave me no food, I was thirsty and you gave me nothing to drink, 43 I was a stranger and you did not welcome me, naked and you did not give me clothing, sick and in prison and you did not visit me." 44 Then they also will answer, "Lord, when was it that we saw you hungry or thirsty or a stranger or naked or sick or in prison, and did not take care of you?" 45 Then he will answer them, "Truly I tell you, just as you did not do it to one of the least of these, you did not do it to me." 46 And these will go away into eternal punishment, but the righteous into eternal life. (NIV)

A few things should be said in explanation of this passage. First, Jesus the judge separates all the people of the earth into two camps, the righteous ("sheep") on his right and the unrighteous ("goats") on his left. This happens before any words of inquiry or judgment are spoken. Second, in the conversation, the two groups do not seem surprised that they did (the sheep) and didn't (the goats) do the things Jesus lists. They *are* surprised that it is to Jesus himself that these things are done or not done. Third, the first time "the least of these" is mentioned, "my brothers and sisters" is added (v. 40); the second time, it is omitted, probably for conciseness (v. 45). However, it is implied in v. 45 because of the first mention. Just as the wording of vv. 42–43 is shortened up in v. 44, but still applies there, so too "my brothers and sisters" is assumed to apply in v. 45. Moreover, "the least of these" used in v. 44 and quoted by itself and out of context doesn't make much sense—the least of these *what*? Fourth, on the whole it's a stark, dramatic picture, even frightening to some, with the only outcomes being salvation or damnation. After Jesus renders his verdict, "They [the condemned] will go away to eternal punishment, but the righteous into eternal life" (v. 46). The point of the whole passage is clear: One's eternal destiny is tied to caring for "the least of these," whoever they are.

Matthew 25 gives few clues as to who "the least of these" are. They're described only as hungry, thirsty, homeless, naked, sick, and imprisoned; the passage doesn't explicitly say why "the least of these" are this way. Two main possibilities have been proposed, a wider and a narrower meaning. The wider meaning is the most common today among Christians and in our culture in general. "The least of these" are the poor, whoever and wherever they might be. Who are more in need of help than the poor, who are hungry, thirsty, homeless, naked, sick, and imprisoned? This option has some current scholarly support and echoes the consistent biblical call to justice for the all the poor. It's easy to see why this understanding of "the least of these" is so championed by justice-minded Christians. It looks accurate as an interpretation of "the least of these," and it is effective in fund-raising campaigns to stir compassion for the poor. Most recently, the Matthew 25 Movement calls on American Christians to sign a pledge to support those "least of these" who are immigrants and refugees.

Despite how persuasive it looks at first, this option runs into problems. First, this passage doesn't say only "the least of these," as this verse is typically quoted. It says more fully in v. 40, "the least of these *my brothers and sisters*." (The Greek actually says "my brothers," but in ancient Greek, "brothers" could also include sisters. The NRSV paraphrases the meaning of "my brothers" as "members of my family.") This wider interpretation of "the least of these" doesn't adequately account for the meaning of "my brothers and sisters." Nowhere else in the teaching of Jesus or in the New Testament in general are all the oppressed and needy of the world called Jesus' "brothers and sisters" or "family." This doesn't mean that "brothers and sisters" can't be used this way only in Matthew 25, but it does make such a use unlikely.

The second, narrower possibility is a much better option for interpreting this verse. The "least of these my brothers" are the least of Jesus' disciples, followers of Jesus who carry his message and meet life-threatening difficulties because of it. Jesus' "brothers and sisters" in the Gospel of Matthew are typically those who believe in him, his followers and disciples. (For example, see Matthew 12:48–50; 28:10). The term "brothers" is used of no one else (except for literal brothers and sisters, of course), and in the New Testament as a whole it means fellow believers. It is not used in the sense so often done today, "fellow human beings." So the "hungry, thirsty, homeless, naked, sick, and imprisoned" people are those of Jesus' disciples who have suffered these hardships.

Another difficulty for the wider interpretation of "the least of these" arises from this text. Caring for the hungry, thirsty, homeless, naked, sick, and imprisoned isn't presented elsewhere in the New Testament as the only measure of obedience to the gospel and the only criterion of judgment at the end of time. However, what *is* presented as a sole criterion of judgment is how people treat Jesus' emissaries and their gospel message. In chapter 10 of Matthew, Jesus says in sending out his twelve disciples to preach his message, "If anyone will not welcome you or listen to your words, shake off the dust from your feet as you leave that house or town. Truly I tell you, it will be more tolerable for the land of Sodom and Gomorrah on the day of judgment than for that town" (Matthew 10:14–15). This judgment on the basis of how people receive the gospel and treat the gospel messengers supports the narrower interpretation of Jesus' oppressed "brothers and sisters" in need.

If this narrower meaning of "the least of these" still seems unlikely to you, here is a parallel to consider. The command "Love one another" is prominent in 1 John, where it is found six times (3:11, 14, 23; 4:7, 11, 12). If "Love one another" is taken alone, it could easily be construed as a wide call to love everyone we come in contact with. This is likely the meaning of "one another" in the expression that the comedian Ellen DeGeneres uses to close her television show: "Be kind to one another." But in the New Testament generally, and always in 1 John, "one another" refers exclusively to people within the church, and "love one another" is an intrachurch command. The New Testament is not opposed to loving of all people, of course—in fact, the New Testament commands it—but that is not the topic or the meaning here. So too in Matthew 25, "the least of these" might seem to apply to everyone, but coupled with "my brothers and sisters" it really refers to oppressed followers of Jesus, his "brothers and sisters" in his faith family.

Do those who misinterpret this verse get anything right about it? First, this passage does indeed command our service to those who are desperately in need of help, although those who hold to the misunderstanding misconstrue who these people are. Second, this passage does in fact contain a strong imperative. God requires meaningful ministry to those Christians who need it the most, and God will reveal to us at the last judgment how well we have done it, or if we have done it at all.

What are the significant takeaways from the corrected understanding of this verse? First, the corrected understanding of this passage underscores the importance of how we treat other Christians who suffer for their efforts to live the faith and spread the faith. Millions of Christians are suffering hunger, illness, imprisonment and other adversities because they live and speak the gospel. Are we showing Christ's love to them in practical ways, in feeding, clothing, welcoming, visiting and comforting them? Or have North American Christians grown complacent about this because we aren't persecuted as they are? This passage says that all the peoples of the earth will be judged according to how they treat the emissaries of Christ, and Christ himself who is with them ("you did it to me"). We cannot answer for how those outside the Christian faith may fare in this judgment, but we can answer for ourselves.

Second, this passage raises the question of the relationship of justification by grace through faith and God's judgment of our works. This is a topic on which there is much current scholarly discussion, and we cannot do it justice here.[1] In brief, we have strong biblical warrant to affirm both: salvation now and in eternity is based on grace alone through faith, *and* God will examine our works at the last judgment. We can wonder about how faith and works are related, but both are affirmed and both are important. As the redeemed enter the kingdom of God after their judgment, they will have a full and accurate knowledge of how well they served their Savior.

Finally, does this corrected understanding of "the least of these" mean that the Bible emphasizes the duty of helping the distressed any less? Not

---

1. For a helpful summary of the options, see Wilkin, *Four Views*.

in the least! All the other biblical injunctions to help them and do justice to them still stand, including the words of Jesus himself. But the cause of all the distressed will not be helped when "the least of these" from Matthew 25 is distorted to make a point that other Bible passages make clearly and well.

QUESTIONS FOR REFLECTION AND DISCUSSION

1. If you have held in the past to the position that this chapter calls a misunderstanding, what do you think about it now that you have considered another interpretation?
2. Some Christians find this passage scary. Why do you think this is? Have you found it frightening or intimidating?
3. What do you think about the relationship of salvation by grace through faith and judgment according to works? Why is it important to affirm both, however they may be related?
4. Give your thoughts on this statement: "Few things can get some Christians to open their checkbooks faster than linking their generosity to their eternal destiny."
5. In the last sermon I heard on this passage, the preacher began by saying, "I want to assure you all that I don't take any of this literally, except the 'least of these' saying." What do you think of such a statement?
6. Ideally, what would be our motivation for caring for "the least of these," whoever they are?

15

What Cross Must We Bear?

If anyone wants to follow me, let him deny himself, take up his cross and follow me. (Mark 8:34)

WHEN THE LATE ROCK star Gregg Allman wrote the story of his life, he titled it *My Cross to Bear*. This refers to his band's 1969 song, "It's Not My Cross to Bear." Allman writes in his book about his several "crosses": strife in the Allman Brothers band, his brother Duane's death at the age of twenty-four in a motorcycle accident, his six difficult marriages splashed over the tabloids, and his long drug and alcohol abuse that led to some permanent effects from disease. Allman's book is both a celebration of his life and a cautionary tale.

Allman's notion of "bearing a cross" reflects the way many people today understand this phrase. "We all have our cross to bear" is a common saying, and a way for people to cope with their troubles in life. A look at current dictionaries will illustrate this. A "cross" is widely known as "any significant trial, affliction or burden," as the *American Heritage Dictionary* defines it. These can be medical, psychological, relational, or financial—in short, almost anything that causes one serious problems, even including self-inflicted difficulties such as "a temper that is her cross." The *Dictionary of Cultural Literacy* says that this important expression typically means "any painful responsibility that is forced upon one."[1] The Dictionary.com

---

1. Hirsch et al., *Dictionary of Cultural Literacy*, 6.

website defines a cross to bear as a "burden or trial one must put up with, as in 'Alzheimer's is a cross to bear for the whole family,' or in a lighter vein, 'Mowing that huge lawn once a week is Brad's cross to bear.'"[2] Finally, the authoritative *Oxford English Dictionary* gives one meaning of a "cross" as "any trouble, vexation or annoyance." It traces the use of "bear one's cross" in written English all the way back to 1573.

This interpretation of "bearing our cross" is a misunderstanding of what Jesus meant by saying, "If anyone wants to come after me, he must deny himself and take up his cross and follow me" (Mark 8:34, NIV; see also the parallels in Matthew 16:24 and Luke 9:23). Our "crosses to bear" are not the ordinary difficulties of life, even when they come to Christians. Chronic illness in the body, mental illness, joblessness, difficult relationships, and many other adversities are indeed heavy burdens in life, and we need God's guidance and strength to deal with them in a faithful way. The Bible assures us that God cares as we go through these things. However, they are not the "cross" that Jesus talks about here. That "cross" comes between the expressions "denying oneself" and "following Jesus" in his self-sacrifice, so it refers to the particular troubles that come when we follow Jesus: temptations to compromise or abandon God, spiritual struggles and disappointments in following Jesus, or opposition and especially persecution because we follow him. These are the kinds of troubles Jesus faced that led to his cross, and for many Christians today following Jesus means being willing to die for him. But "bearing our cross" doesn't mean dealing with the usual troubles of life, some of which, as Gregg Allman did, we bring upon ourselves by our own foolish choices. If there is one thing that Christians shouldn't trivialize by misunderstanding a Bible verse, it is Jesus bearing his cross for us.

A look at this verse in its context in Mark, Matthew, and Luke shows that this is the meaning. The passage immediately before this verse has Jesus asking his disciples: "Who do people say I am?" When they answer, he asks more pointedly, "Who do *you* say I am?" Peter speaks for the disciples when he answers, "You are the Christ." Then Jesus teaches them, in the first prediction of three, about his suffering, death, and resurrection. These predicted events show what kind of Messiah Jesus will be: one who denies himself, picks up his cross, and faithfully follows God's plan. Mark 8 continues:

> 31 He then began to teach them that the Son of Man must suffer many things and be rejected by the elders, the chief priests and the

---

2. Dictionary.com, "Cross to Bear."

teachers of the law, and that he must be killed and after three days rise again. ³² He spoke plainly about this, and Peter took him aside and began to rebuke him. ³³ But when Jesus turned and looked at his disciples, he rebuked Peter. "Get behind me, Satan!" he said. "You do not have in mind the concerns of God, but merely human concerns."

³⁴ Then he called the crowd to him along with his disciples and said: "Whoever wants to be my disciple must deny themselves and take up their cross and follow me. ³⁵ For whoever wants to save their life will lose it, but whoever loses their life for me and for the gospel will save it. ³⁶ What good is it for someone to gain the whole world, yet forfeit their soul? ³⁷ Or what can anyone give in exchange for their soul? ³⁸ If anyone is ashamed of me and my words in this adulterous and sinful generation, the Son of Man will be ashamed of them when he comes in his Father's glory with the holy angels." (NIV)

Jesus' disciples, however, don't understand that their teacher will be a suffering, and crucified, Messiah. Peter takes Jesus aside for a private rebuke. Perhaps Peter believes that rebuking Jesus privately rather than publicly will cause Jesus to rethink the goals of his ministry and mission. Then Jesus rebukes Peter in view of the other disciples. Jesus rejects Peter's refusal to recognize God's plan for Jesus to lay down his life. Jesus then calls the crowd and his disciples, and says that those who wish to follow him must deny self. This denying one's self involves continuous repentance and a total commitment to live for Jesus only, to the point of possible martyrdom.

Then comes taking up one's cross. It was a common practice that each one condemned to crucifixion "carry his cross" from place of judgment to the place of execution. The disciples probably hear Jesus' words literally since they had no basis for understanding them symbolically, and they wonder if they will be dying with their teacher. This whole message must have been astounding to the disciples: Jesus was not only going to die soon, but he would die by execution; and, if that weren't enough, Jesus was calling them to join him in this self-sacrifice!

What is the significance for our Christian life today of the corrected understanding of "bearing our cross"? First, according to our corrected understanding, bearing a cross involves a personal decision and action, which is obscured by some newer translations. The NRSV and the NIV, probably in an effort to avoid male-oriented language, starts with the singular "if anyone" but then switches to plurals: "deny *themselves* and take up *their* cross and follow me." This may imply to some readers that the actions Jesus calls for here are group actions. But this verse is in the singular in the Greek original, not in the plural, so these plurals could be misleading here, especially to those not familiar with this recent translational practice. (The false plurals continue through verse 38.) What is the significance of all these singulars? They imply that to deny oneself and take up one's cross, following Jesus' own decision in obedience to God's will and plan, is each believer's personal decision. We often make this decision in the church, in a family, or other group, but the process is also an unavoidably individual task.

Second, the nuances of the Greek verbs are important in Mark 8:34, and come through only partially in the English translations. "Deny" and "take up" are a type of Greek command that generally denotes a single action. This implies that Jesus views denying oneself and taking up one's cross as a single decision leading to a one-time action. We might view them as needing to be done constantly, and there is some truth in that. Luke suggests this by adding "daily" to "take up your cross" (9:23), but the single-action aspect comes across in Mark and Matthew. All following of Jesus begins with a decision to do so, and this involves denying oneself and picking up one's cross. "Follow," on the other hand, is a present-tense command that implies continuous action. We follow Jesus, and keep on following him, in his way of self-denial and self-giving.

Third, this verse gives a clear insight into the cost of discipleship. Salvation is free, a matter of God's sheer grace given to us in the death and resurrection of Jesus. However, following Jesus is costly. It involves a self-denial that is willing to give up our own life in ways big and small. The picking-up of our cross is a willingness to endure suffering, and to follow Jesus in ways that lead through death to life. We are helped by knowing that we are following the example of Jesus here. There was no Christ without the cross, so there should be no Christian without a cross.

QUESTIONS FOR REFLECTION AND DISCUSSION

1. Have you heard or used the expression "bear the cross" as the misunderstanding of this verse does? If so, what do you think about the phrase now?

What Cross Must We Bear?

2. How does "take up his cross daily" in Luke 9:23 correspond to what Mark and Matthew imply about the one-time action of taking up one's cross?

3. What do you think Jesus' disciples thought, not only when they heard him speak for the first time in Mark of his own death by crucifixion, but also when they heard Jesus' call for the disciples themselves to "bear the cross"?

4. What might be the implications of "follow" being a continuous action verb?

5. What does it look like for today's Christian in America to "take up his/her cross" and follow Jesus?

6. Although "bear one's cross" is not about ordinary suffering, still the phrase leads us to ask, how do we handle the ordinary troubles of life?

16

Is "The Poor You Have with You Always" a Directive?

The poor you have with you always. (Mark 14:7)

THIS VERSE IS NOT one of the most popular verses in the Bible, given its difficult topic. I doubt if many Christians with a "life verse" have chosen this one. However, it is often appealed to, although it is misunderstood and misapplied. "The poor you have with you always" is used by some Christians in modern times to justify doing little or nothing personally to help the poor, especially when this help is designed to end their poverty. It carries a lot of weight for them, since Jesus himself said it. "Jesus told us that the poor will always be here," they contend, "so we can't eliminate poverty. This situation may not be nice, but it's clearly God's will. So don't fight it." Sometimes people quote this verse as an excuse to avoid asking hard questions about poverty or discussing it at all. At other times this objection is directed at church or parachurch efforts against poverty. More often it is directed against government programs for the poor, which can be controversial. "The poor you have with you always," some people repeat, "so government efforts to help the poor are bound to be unsuccessful because they go against God's will."

The narrative from the life of Jesus in which this saying is found will make clear that this is a misunderstanding of "the poor you have with you always." This account must have been told often in the first years of

Christianity, since it is found in Matthew (26:6–13), Mark (14:3–9), and John (12:1–8). It is also found in Luke 7:36–50, but Luke omits this saying "the poor you have with you always." Here is the passage from Mark 14:

> 3 While he was at Bethany in the house of Simon the leper, as he sat at the table, a woman came with an alabaster jar of very costly ointment of nard, and she broke open the jar and poured the ointment on his head. 4 But some were there who said to one another in anger, "Why was the ointment wasted in this way? 5 For this ointment could have been sold for more than three hundred denarii, and the money given to the poor." And they scolded her. 6 But Jesus said, "Let her alone; why do you trouble her? She has performed a good service for me. 7 For you always have the poor with you, and you can show kindness to them whenever you wish; but you will not always have me. 8 She has done what she could; she has anointed my body beforehand for its burial. 9 Truly I tell you, wherever the good news is proclaimed in the whole world, what she has done will be told in remembrance of her."

A most important thing to know in this passage is that Jesus is using Deuteronomy 15:11, "The poor will never cease out of the land" (KJV; this is a literal translation of the Hebrew). Jesus often alludes to the Old Testament, and many of those listening to this saying would recognize its origins in Deuteronomy. We should consider this saying in its Deuteronomy context:

> 7 If there is among you anyone in need, a member of your community in any of your towns within the land that the LORD your God is giving you, do not be hard-hearted or tight-fisted toward your needy neighbor. 8 You should rather open your hand, willingly lending enough to meet the need, whatever it may be. 9 Be careful that you do not entertain a mean thought, thinking, "The seventh year, the year of remission, is near," and therefore view your needy neighbor with hostility and give nothing; your neighbor might cry to the LORD against you, and you would incur guilt. 10 Give liberally and be ungrudging when you do so, for on this account the LORD your God will bless you in all your work and in all that you undertake. 11 Since there will never cease to be some in need on the earth, I therefore command you, "Open your hand to the poor and needy neighbor in your land."

Deuteronomy points out a sad but true situation: there will always be some people at the low end of the economic spectrum, who will be poor and needy in some sense. This was true even in ancient Israel, with its ideas of land ownership for all families, interest-free loans, just wages for all laborers, and freedom for Israelite slaves every seven years. The reasons for the continued existence of poverty are not given here, or even hinted at. Other parts of the Old Testament occasionally imply that poverty is a result of laziness. Much more often it attributes poverty to oppression by the rich and powerful through various means (holding back daily wages, ruinous taxation, land seizures, and so forth), and at still other times poverty results from famine. Despite poverty's varied causes, and despite its persistence, Deuteronomy 15 affirms that doing good for the poor is more than an opportunity: it is a necessity. God says emphatically, "I therefore command you, 'Open your hand to the poor and needy neighbor in your land.'" To use "the poor you have with you always" to refuse to help the poor is exactly contrary to the central point of what both Deuteronomy and Jesus are saying.

This misunderstanding is another example of quoting out of context, one of the leading causes of misunderstanding the Bible. In the case of "the poor you have with you always," not even the whole sentence is quoted! This partial and noncontextual quotation leads immediately to a glaring misunderstanding and misuse of this verse. For people who know the whole verse, the true meaning of "the poor you have with you always" comes clear. Jesus is telling his disciples that they always have an opportunity and obligation to help the poor, but at the moment Jesus said this, it was more important to honor him.

The fact that Deuteronomy and Jesus envision social systems where poverty is more or less a permanent part of life makes some Christians uncomfortable. Probably most everyone would like to see poverty and its pernicious effects on human life ended. Some people believe the lofty rhetoric of President John F. Kennedy's 1960 inaugural address in which he said, "Man holds in his mortal hands the power to abolish all forms of human poverty." Nevertheless, it is a misunderstanding to take Jesus' saying as a directive. Jesus doesn't say "The poor you *must* have with you always" or "The poor you have with you always, so your efforts for them are wasted." His words don't mean that Christians should automatically distrust any effort to lift the poor, or withhold charity from them. To do so is ignore the implications of Jesus' words, and the main point of Deuteronomy 15:7–11. In fact, using this misunderstood verse to justify not helping the poor sets us in exact opposition to Jesus. Even when we realize that our efforts may

Is "The Poor You Have with You Always" a Directive?

not end poverty and that the poor will indeed be with us always, we are still under a divine command to help them as best we can. Not to do so will cause the poor to "cry to God against us."

Is there any part of this misunderstanding that is correct? Only a little, but it is important. Jesus is indeed saying that there will always be some people who are poor. In this fallen world, turned away from God, social inequalities will always exist to some extent, no matter what our economic system. Only the return of Jesus and the reign of God it brings will end all poverty of mind, spirit, and possessions. (Deuteronomy 15:4–5 says that if the people of Israel keep God's law fully, there will not be a needy person among them. God's intention is that no one should live in poverty.) Because human sin has a role in creating and perpetuating poverty, poverty sadly will exist as long as this present age exists. But the reason Jesus says this is not to forbid efforts to help the poor, as the misuse of this verse claims.

What are some implications of the corrected understanding of this verse for us today? First, it should be said that Christians who agree on helping the poor can disagree on the best way to do so. Jesus does not lay down here, or anywhere else for that matter, a detailed political, social, or economic program to help the poor. This is something he leaves to us, expecting that we will be guided by what the Word says and how the Holy Spirit leads us to apply that Word.

A second consideration from this verse is this: it's often easier for Christians to be generous toward the poor in other lands than in their own land. This is why denominations and mission agencies can more effectively raise money for "world relief" in Africa and Asia than for relief here at home. That's not what Deuteronomy and Jesus envisioned, because they speak of "the neighbor" (Deuteronomy) and "the poor with you" (Jesus). The closer poor people are to us (our "neighbors" and those "with us"), the more they should be the ones we help. In particular, we should help the poor within our own churches, our brothers and sisters in faith, as the New Testament illustrates and even commands. For example, see Galatians 6:10: "Therefore, as we have opportunity, let us do good to all people, especially to those who belong to the family of believers" (NIV); see also James 2:14–16. The command to help the poor is found widely in the Old Testament as well. To cite two examples in addition to Deuteronomy 15, Proverbs depicts the virtuous woman: "She opens her arms to the poor and extends her hands to the needy" (Proverbs 31:20). Ezekiel 18:7 says of the righteous man, "He does not oppress anyone, but returns what he took in pledge for a loan. He does not commit robbery but gives his food to the hungry and provides clothing for the naked."

Finally, we must notice that the Bible speaks here of "the poor." The Bible has abstract words such as "poverty," but it doesn't often use them. In the Bible, poverty is not an abstract, conceptual social or economic issue. Instead, it's a matter of *people*: "*The poor* you have with you always, and you can help *them* anytime you want." In sum, we would understand Jesus' message in this verse better if we see "the poor you have with you always" as affirming Deuteronomy, and if we focused our action on carrying out the command to "do good to them."

QUESTIONS FOR REFLECTION AND DISCUSSION

1. Why, in your opinion, are there so many poor people in the world?
2. In your own words, what is the point of Jesus' statement about the poor?
3. What are some of the challenges and disagreements the church faces in addressing poverty?
4. Have you had your own struggles in knowing how to help the poor? If so, what are these struggles, and how have you responded to them?
5. Although American Christians give generously to crisis needs such as famines in Africa and storm damage in Haiti, this crisis-response giving is gradually taking the place of regular giving for long-term change. What might be problematic about this?
6. What do you sense God calling you toward in this study?

17

Who Is a Good Samaritan?

But a Samaritan while travelling came near him; when he saw him, he was moved with pity. He went to him, poured oil and wine on his wounds, and bandaged them. Then he put him on his own animal, brought him to an inn, and took care of him. (Luke 10:33–34)

THE COMMON EXPRESSION "A good Samaritan," meaning someone who helps a stranger in need, comes from the parable of the Good Samaritan in Luke 10. Although it's told only in Luke, many Christians think of it as one of Jesus' most important parables. Most North Americans are familiar with the phrase "good Samaritan" and use it in everyday life. The *American Heritage Dictionary* defines a "good Samaritan" as a "compassionate person who unselfishly helps others." Many hospitals and charitable organizations in North America are named after the Good Samaritan. A "Good Sam Club" of recreational-vehicle owners calls on its members to aid travelers in trouble on the roads. Most states have laws that offer legal protection to passersby who aid people in trouble, protections that are known as Good Samaritan laws. Now "Good Samaritan" is such a common phrase that "Samaritan" can even stand by itself for "Good Samaritan," as in Samaritan's Purse, the name of a Christian humanitarian relief organization.

A close look at the parable and its context will bring it into focus and make clear its correct, full meaning. Jesus is asked by an expert in the law of Moses, "Who is my neighbor?" (Luke 10:29). This was not a flippant question, because there was a good deal of debate in first-century Judaism about the meaning of "neighbor" in commands such as "love your neighbor as yourself" (Leviticus 19:18). As he sometimes does, Jesus answers a question with a parable. The person who asked the question must listen to the parable and in a sense get inside the story to figure out Jesus' answer to the question. In the parable an unidentified man is going from Jerusalem to Jericho. Some interpreters think that he is a human with no explicit national identity, but it is most likely that Jesus' hearers would assume that this man was Jewish, as the majority of travelers on this Judean road probably were. Moreover, when Jesus begins a parable with "a man" or "a woman," it typically implies a *Jewish* person. Jesus' earthly ministry is primarily to his own people, so non-Jews (such as this Samaritan) in Jesus' teaching and in the gospels generally, are explicitly labeled as such.

Now let's continue with the parable. Bandits set upon this man, overpowering him and taking his possessions, even the clothing he is wearing. Not content with this, they beat him senseless and leave him "half dead" in the roadway. A Jewish priest and a Levite (a minor temple official) both come upon this injured person as they travel on that road, but they "pass by on the other side" of the road. They keep as far away as they can. Jesus doesn't give their motivation for refusing to help: Are they motivated by fear of ritual contamination, by fear that the robbers may still be nearby and attack them if they stop, or perhaps by unwillingness to "get involved," as we say today? We naturally wonder what motivated them not to help, and many preachers have exploited these supposed motivations, but the point is that these two Jewish men didn't help, despite the biblical commands to help one's fellow countrymen in dire need. Then a Samaritan travelling on that road saw him and "was moved with pity." His compassion moved him to do something the others didn't: he tended the man's wounds, put him on his own animal, brought him to an inn, and personally tended to him through the night. The next day the Samaritan paid the innkeeper to continue this care and promised to reimburse him for further expenses. The parable being ended, Jesus asks the expert in the law, "Which of these do you think was a neighbor to the man who fell into the hands of robbers?" The expert knows the answer: "The one who showed him mercy." Jesus responds, "Go and do likewise"; in other words, be a neighbor like that.

We misunderstand this parable by thinking of the Samaritan only as an example of love and care for a stranger. In particular, we underinterpret it by grasping only half of its truth. The "Good Samaritan" in Jesus' teaching is not just any helpful stranger, but a particular kind of stranger: one who belongs to the enemies of God's chosen people, and one whose people saw the Jews as enemies. Showing love to people we don't know is a deeply Christian action, of course, because it falls within the scope of the gospel command to do good to all people. In Jesus' parable, a Samaritan is a surprising, completely unexpected person who helps a stranger in need. Even in trouble a Jew would distrust a Samaritan, probably refusing Samaritan help. (The fact that the robbed man is "half dead" probably means that he can't object to help from this Samaritan even if he wants to.) In sum, the parable of the Good Samaritan is a narrative example of Jesus' command to "love your enemies" (Matthew 5:43–48), because the enemy can be a neighbor, too.

To understand how Jews and Samaritans were such enemies, we must look at their common history. Hostility between Jews and Samaritans went back a long time before Jesus, almost seven hundred years, in fact. The Samaritans claimed to be descendants of the tribes of the Northern Kingdom. Josephus, the first-century Jewish historian, wrote that foreigners brought into Northern Kingdom of Israel after its takeover by the Assyrian Empire in 722 BCE became the ancestors of the Samaritans. They supposedly intermarried with Israelite survivors of this invasion. Josephus also states that they built a temple in Samaria around 200 BCE, which the Jewish ruler John Hyrcanus destroyed around 100 BCE, increasing hostilities. In one particularly dastardly incident, Samaritans scattered human bones in the Jewish temple in Jerusalem in an effort to defile it. The New Testament gives a more mixed perspective on Samaritans. Right before the chapter containing the parable of the Good Samaritan, Luke records that Jesus, a Jew, had trouble in Samaritan villages (9:52–53), and in the Gospel of Matthew Jesus commanded his disciples not to go to Samaria during his ministry (10:5–6). However, Jesus entered Samaria and talked with a Samaritan woman, a conversation that laid a foundation of faith in Jesus that profoundly affected many people in her city (John 4:1–42). Jesus healed a Samaritan leper who proved to be grateful when Jewish lepers were not (Luke 17:11–19). The Great Commission at the end of Matthew commands mission to "all nations/peoples," which includes Samaritans (28:19). Many Samaritans became a part of the growing church (Acts 8:4–25). In general, though, Jews looked on Samaritans as heretics, in some ways as worse than Gentiles, and for Samaritans the feelings of suspicion and dislike were mutual. This makes clear how Jesus' original followers, and in particular this expert in the law of Moses, would have heard the term "Samaritan" in this parable: a Samaritan was a member of an enemy nation and religion. A Samaritan would be the last person they would expect to show mercy to the victim, and his actions make him a "Good" Samaritan because he acts in mercy toward an injured man who belongs to an enemy group.

What's right in the misunderstanding corrected in this chapter? Quite a bit, actually. Unlike several of the misunderstood verses we are considering in this study, this passage is not completely ripped out of its context, quoted incorrectly, or otherwise misused. This parable does indeed urge love for a stranger in need. It urges us to feel pity toward those "beaten up" in life, both literally and figuratively, and to act on this pity to help them. Nothing in a corrected understanding of this parable means that we should give any less of this help to anyone, whether friend, foe, or perfect stranger. But what makes the traditional popular view of this parable a misunderstanding is that it doesn't go far enough and deep enough. It's not primarily love for a stranger that's spoken of here, as the common understanding of the Good Samaritan's action would have it. Instead, it is love for a stranger *who is an enemy*. The enemy is also a neighbor, Jesus says.

The takeaway from this corrected understanding is illustrated well in a recent incident in San Francisco. Late at night, a man speeding down a street lost control of his car; it spun wildly and crashed. The driver was trapped inside, and his car started to burn. Three passersby hesitated for a second and then jumped into action, ignoring the danger to themselves from a possible car explosion. When they couldn't open the car doors to get the man out, they cleverly used a sign post that the car had broken off to smash in the car's windows, allowing the smoke to exit and the man inside to breathe. The police and firefighters arrived soon to extricate this man, and they said that the actions of these three had saved his life. This man, it turns out, was Arabian, which was evident from his clothing. Those who assisted him saw this before helping him. They may have carried the same initial suspicion or wariness that some Americans have about Arabians after 9/11, and they didn't know if he was a visitor or an American citizen, but they saved him anyway. They were true "Good Samaritans" to the driver because they treated the injured man as one of their own people. Jesus' final word for us is the same he gave the expert in the law of Moses who questioned him: "Go and do likewise."

QUESTIONS FOR REFLECTION AND DISCUSSION

1. What do you think of when you hear the term "Good Samaritan"?
2. How does understanding the relationship between Jews and Samaritans change the impact of Jesus' parable?
3. Who are your/our "Samaritans" today?
4. Have you ever had the opportunity to help a personal enemy? What did you do? How did that affect you and your relationships?
5. What might this parable say about being helped by those we think of as enemies?
6. What might it mean for us to "Go and do likewise"?

18

How Did God Give His Only Son?

For God so loved the world that he gave his only Son, so that everyone who believes in him may not perish but may have eternal life. (John 3:16)

FOR MANY CHRISTIANS TODAY, John 3:16 summarizes the Christian faith. They have good company in doing so; Martin Luther, the sixteenth-century leader of the Protestant Reformation, called John 3:16 "the Gospel in miniature." More Christians know this verse by memory than probably any other. Websites featuring the text of the Bible typically report that it is the most looked-up verse in the Bible. Some people use it as an evangelistic tool, writing only "John 3:16"—not even its words!—on signs, walls, and so forth, to draw attention to this verse. They hope that some people will recognize this as a Bible reference, look up the verse, take it to heart, and come to faith in Jesus Christ. The In-N-Out Burger restaurant chain prints "John 3:16" on the inside of the bottom rim of their paper cups. The clothing company Forever 21 prints it on their shopping bags. When he played college football, Tim Tebow often printed "John 3:16" in his eye black. All these are trying in their own way to witness to the gospel, thinking that people might read this verse and take it to heart.

Sometimes people misunderstand Bible verses by seeing only half the meaning in them. What they see in a verse isn't wrong, but it is incomplete, so the verse is not as meaningful as it should be. John 3:16 is such a verse. Despite being the most loved and the most thought about verse in the Bible, it is only partially understood by many Christians because it is not read in its context. The misunderstanding involves the word "gave." If we understand John 3:16 on its own and ignore the verses around it, "God so loved the world" shapes "that he gave his only Son" into the implied meaning "God gave his Son to the world." As we will see below, this loses the more precise nuance that "gave" has in its John 3 context, "gave up to death." Someone summarized this verse to me in a way that illustrates this misunderstanding: "God loves people so much that he gave his Son to this sinful world, so all who believe in Jesus will live eternally." This summary of John 3:16 completely glosses over the significance of Jesus' death as the basis of salvation.

Since this verse does not mention the death of Jesus explicitly, it's easy to see how this misunderstanding could develop. This "giving to the world" meaning focuses on Jesus' incarnation and presence in the world, which is a strong theme in John from its beginning. However, just as important in the Gospel of John, and in the Christian gospel in general, is the belief that the Son was sent by his Father into the world to die for us. God didn't give his Son only to become human and live here, to teach us more directly and personally God's way. This is not the gospel as traditionally understood. The "gospel in miniature" in John 3:16, seen in context, says this: God gave his Son to the world both to live and die for us. Christ's incarnation is for the ultimate purpose of his death and resurrection.

Let's take a closer look at this verse, phrase by phrase. In "For God so loved the world" we have a statement that ties this verse to the sentences preceding it with "for." "So loved" may refer to a quantity of love ("so much") or a quality of love ("in such a way"). New Testament scholars differ right down the middle on this quantity/quality issue because the wording is ambiguous, and the author of John could be deliberately ambiguous here in order to include both. At any rate, the assertion that God loved the world makes the beginning of this verse very appealing to modern people. The next phrase, "that he gave," we will reserve for special treatment in the next paragraph. Next in this verse comes the object of "gave," "his only Son." In older translations of the Bible, "only" is rendered "only begotten." In several recent translations, a footnote is used to point to this as a possible translation. "Only Son" language connects with the teaching in John 1 that Jesus is the only Son of God, who existed before the world began and became human in Jesus of Nazareth. This is another reason why "gave" here is often restricted to "gave to the world." Most commentators point to a clear reference in "only Son" to Abraham's obedient offering of his only son Isaac in

Genesis 22. In the middle of this verse, "so that" indicates that God's purpose was to bring salvation to the world with the giving of his Son. Finally, the end of this verse, "everyone who believes in him may not perish but may have eternal life," stresses the necessity of personal faith. Faith makes the benefit of the life and death of Jesus—eternal life—effective.

Now we need to look even closer at "gave," which is at the heart of the misunderstanding of this verse. As we suggested above, "gave" in the context of John 3:16 includes the death of the Son, not just his incarnation. God gave the Son to the world, and God gave him up to death. John 3:16 starts with a "for," which means that it has a strong connection with vv. 14–15. Verse 16 explains that the crucifixion of Jesus, his "lifting up" (v. 14) is done out of God's love for the world and as a part of the giving of the Son. This "lifting up" is an obvious reference to the death of Jesus on the cross, but many interpreters also see a strong hint of the resurrection of Jesus in "lifted up." (In fact, John may see "lifting up" of Jesus as the whole sequence of events: death, resurrection, and ascension.) What is more, the strikingly similar wording draws vv. 15 and 16 together: v. 15 states "whoever believes in him may have eternal life," and v. 16 states "everyone who believes in him may not perish but may have eternal life." The English varies slightly here, but the wording in Greek for "whoever/everyone who believes in him may have eternal life" in these two verses is exactly the same. As a result, when we read John 3:16 with vv. 14 and 15, there is no way we can avoid seeing the strong connection of "he gave his only Son" with the lifting up of Jesus on the cross.

Why is this famous verse typically not seen in context so that its full meaning can be more easily understood? The main reason is common in misunderstood verses: some verses are thought to be so clear and powerful on their own that they don't need any help from their context. People often think that John 3:16 is completely intelligible on its own. However, like all texts, John 3:16 has a context, and as we have seen, this context makes a difference in its meaning. Another reason this verse is often taken out of context has to do with the way modern Bibles arrange John 3. In the New Revised Standard Version (NRSV), just as in the Revised Standard Version (RSV), John 3:16 not only starts a new paragraph, but it is a whole paragraph! This one-sentence paragraph is very unusual, even odd, for Bible translations. In setting John 3:16 as its own paragraph, the translators may aim to give extra prominence to it, but this typographical decision contributes to the misunderstanding that the verse can stand alone. Verse 16 either should be kept with the previous paragraph (vv. 11–15), as in a few English versions, or should become the first sentence of the next paragraph, as in the New International Version (NIV, vv. 17–21).

What is the significance for today of this deeper meaning of John 3:16? First, as we have seen above, the gospel, even in its John 3:16 miniature form, covers the whole sweep of Jesus, explicitly or implicitly: his coming to earth, his life, his death, and his resurrection. Every one of these stages is important. It is quite common among more liberal American Protestants to emphasize the teaching of Jesus, and among more conservative Protestants to emphasize his atoning death. Actually, we need both. If we minimize or deny any major aspect of Jesus as presented in the Gospels, we minimize our faith in significant ways. Knowing the full meaning of John 3:16 will help us appreciate the fullness of Jesus' actions for us.

Second, we should deal with the question of who speaks the words of John 3:16. The NRSV presents them as the words of Jesus all the way through v. 21, but then adds a footnote to verse 21 that says, "Some interpreters hold that the quotation concludes with verse 15." The NIV and the English Standard Version (ESV) do the same. All modern translations have to deal with this, because the Greek language of the New Testament didn't use quotation marks, so if the wording is not clear on this, it's not always possible to tell when a quotation ends and narration resumes. Is this important, or just a technical matter that scholars puzzle over? The answer depends on one's view of biblical inspiration. Are the words of John 3:16–21 more true or important if Jesus said them? For those Christians with what I call a "red-letter mentality" (some Bibles print the words of Jesus in red, to make them stand out), these words would indeed be more important if Jesus said them. Someone once said to me that it is important that Jesus spoke John 3:16: "Jesus himself says that only those who trust and believe in Him will have eternal life." But I don't think so. The Christian church as a whole has never had a view of the Bible that says that some words are truer than others, even though Christians naturally have an emotional attachment to Jesus' words. All the words of John 3 are fully true, and truly inspired. John 3:16, read in its context, is a powerful expression of the gospel whether Jesus spoke these words or not.

Finally, this passage shows us that eternal life begins now. It's not something that comes only when we die and go to heaven, as many Christians suppose. In John 3, "judgment" is now for all people in the way they respond to Jesus, "perish" is now, and "have eternal life" is now. Eternal life is present now in us in a partial, anticipatory way, of course, but its presence is significant. We will experience the fullness of life at the end of time, when we and all the creation will be made new. When we believe in Jesus, thus "lifting him up" in our own lives, we have already entered eternal life.

QUESTIONS FOR REFLECTION AND DISCUSSION

1. If this is one of your favorite verses in the Bible, why this is that so?
2. In what ways is this verse a summary of the gospel for you?
3. This verse in its context does not touch on the coming of Jesus at the end of time, which in the New Testament and today is an essential Christian teaching. In light of this, can we really say that John 3:16 is the whole gospel in miniature?
4. What do you think about billboards and other signs that say only "John 3:16"? Is it effective for people to witness to Christ by holding up "John 3:16" signs?
5. Did you have a "red letter Bible" in the past, or have one now? What does this red lettering mean to you? Why, in your opinion, are only the *words* of Jesus printed in red, and not his *deeds*?
6. Read 1 John 4:8–10. How might this passage help to illuminate the fuller meaning of John 3:16?

19

Should We Have All Possessions in Common?

All who believed were together and had all things in common. (Acts 2:44)

THE EARLY CHAPTERS OF the Acts of the Apostles speak about the remarkable community life of the first church in Jerusalem. This church had a full complement of mutually respectful leaders, experienced remarkable numerical and spiritual growth, and lived in harmony with those Jews who did not believe in Jesus as Messiah. It appears to have been an ideal church, and even when sin entered (with deception by Ananias and Sapphira [Acts 5]), it was discovered and dealt with decisively. One facet of their community life that has always fascinated Christians is the practice of sharing possessions among believers. This sharing was so complete, Acts relates, that there was not a single poor person in the earliest church (4:34), a feature that looks back to Deuteronomy 15:4–5: if the people of Israel keep God's law fully, there will not be a needy person among them. This practice as a whole seems to have ended quickly in the first century; at least we have no other mention of it in the later parts of the New Testament. The medieval church in both Eastern Orthodoxy and Roman Catholicism claimed that this practice continued in monasticism, as men who wanted to enter the monastery were usually required to sell their possessions and give them to the poor.

The understanding of this practice today varies among Christians, who are influenced in part by their political views. On the right side of the spectrum, some have seen this as an endorsement of a private-property system with a dose of purely voluntary charity. On the left side of the spectrum, some believe that Jesus' teaching of God's "preferential option for the poor" entails a religious socialism of sorts, and that "all things common" means a redistribution of private possessions. Some interpreters have provocatively called this system of radical sharing "Christian communism." In short, these misunderstandings of "All who believed were together and had all things in common" are frequent among Christians today, among both conservatives and liberals.

What type of sharing did take place in the earliest church, and what might this mean for us today? To answer that question, we should first consider here the two passages from Acts that touch on this subject:

> [2:44] All the believers were together and had everything in common. [45] They sold property and possessions to give to anyone who had need. . . . [4:32] All the believers were one in heart and mind. No one claimed that any of their possessions was their own, but they shared everything they had. [33] With great power the apostles continued to testify to the resurrection of the Lord Jesus. And God's grace was so powerfully at work in them all [34] that there were no needy persons among them. For from time to time those who owned land or houses sold them, brought the money from the sales [35] and put it at the apostles' feet, and it was distributed to anyone who had need. (NIV)

Immediately following this second passage are two contrasting examples of sharing. The story of Barnabas (4:36–37) is a positive example of sincere generosity, and quickly told. The dramatic story about Ananias and Sapphira is a negative example of deceptive generosity that comes to a fatal conclusion (5:1–11).

A careful reading of Acts 1–5 shows that "were together" and "having all things in common" are not to be taken too literally. Some of this misunderstanding can be traced to the way that Luke writes. At times he introduces a new topic by describing it in sweeping terms, then comes back to it a bit later to provide more detail that may alter its introduction. This is a sophisticated way to write, but it can easily lead to misunderstanding when readers don't take in the whole topic; this is one reason for the misunderstanding of Acts 4:32. "Were together" in 2:44 does not mean communal living, despite its appeal to a small number of Christians today who live in communal house churches. Instead, it probably refers to the daily gathering of the church in the courts of the Jerusalem temple, a gathering described by the similar phrase "spent much time together" (Acts 2:46). "Were together" is such a general expression that it could also refer to spiritual unity. Luke also emphasizes the sharing of goods to make a point. As the two stories of Barnabas and of Ananias and Sapphira make clear (Acts 4:36—5:11), giving to the church was need-based and intermittent. Members of the early community continued to own possessions, and the more well-to-do among them lived in their own houses. Luke's point is that they shared freely and fully when a need arose, even to the point of selling property and giving the proceeds to the community. The selling of property was not mandatory, but there was a high expectation for it. As Peter told Ananias, in what had to be the most ominous audit ever, "While it remained unsold, did it not remain your own? And after it was sold, was it not at your disposal?" (Acts 5:4).

Some have asked why there was such a need in the early Jerusalem church. Perhaps a significant number of early believers lived in an endemic poverty not caused by any recent economic changes. Jesus was well loved by ordinary people, many of whom lived in poverty and likely came into the early church. Perhaps crops were poor, so that famine was sweeping through the region. Persecution does happen later, when the apostle Paul raises money from his churches in Greece for the relief of famine-stricken believers in Judea (Acts 11:27–30). Was there also persecution at the time, which may have caused poverty for some and necessitated sharing? Some scholars have said so, but Acts says that the early church was "in favor with all the people" (2:47), so this is not a likely factor here.

What do those who misunderstand this verse get right about it? They are correct that sharing all goods is indeed a radical system; it is not a system that accommodates easily to the way Christians live today. However, calling this a "communist" or even a "socialist" system is improper. The ancient world wasn't capitalist or communist as we know these terms, and neither was the church. Capitalism and communism are modern economic systems with their own ideologies, not systems known in the ancient world.

What are the implications of this corrected understanding for today? First, this radical sharing still serves as a good model for Christians today, and a challenging one. "There was not a needy person among them" carries out the intent of Jesus' statement, "You always have an opportunity to help [the poor]" (Mark 14:7; see chapter 16, above.) This passage is a glimpse into a kingdom-of-God society that the church can realize in part here and now. In times of rising economic inequality, many people in our churches have become poor, or nearly poor. Are we willing to dig deep into our resources to help, and do so in a creative way that lifts people out of their needs? Or might we, like Ananias and Sapphira, pay lip service to generosity so that our greed hurts those who in need?

Second, we should notice carefully that this giving and receiving is within the Christian community. Those outside the Christian community are not expected to give, nor are they the recipients of its funds in this case. On the other hand, we should not be too restrictive in this. The book of Acts does not mean to imply that such a system is only a practice within congregations. Rather, the giving and receiving happened between all those who followed the Christian faith at that time.

Third, there is a downside to the kind of need-based giving many Christians do today. It's relatively easy for churches to raise money for famine or disaster relief, especially when these dire needs appear in the news. But this need-based generosity too often competes with steady, everyday generosity. For example, a large response to disastrous famines often means that it is more difficult to raise money to work for economic development that might help to end famines. Professional fundraisers know that giving for a capital campaign or a special-needs appeal can negatively impact giving for regular, ongoing needs such as an annual operating budget. In a church that aspires to be like so-called New Testament Christians, there should be a desire to meet both immediate and ongoing needs.

Fourth, the radical system of giving that we see in the first chapters of Acts soon disappears from view in the New Testament. It still has a strong appeal to some Christians, however. Many people urge us to practice the "radical generosity" of Acts today. How can this be done today, given our different economic and financial systems? The system of early Acts may not be reproducible for us today, but it's still possible to give generously. One thing we can and should do is start at the beginning, with the basic New Testament foundation of generosity—tithing our income, a full 10 percent (Matthew 23:23). Building on this foundation of generosity enables us to understand that it is only God who owns the world and its wealth. We are its stewards, and we are called to radical generosity.

Finally, the opening of this chapter raised the issue of "Christian communism," which is often mentioned when the earliest church in Acts is discussed. This phrase raises the larger, important issue of the relationship of Christianity and communism. Despite the fall of communist systems in Russian and Eastern Europe, and the mixing of communist political control with free market economics in China, Marxism as the materialist system of thought and economic life that gave birth to communism is still remarkably popular. This is especially true in universities. Public opinion polls have shown that Americans in their twenties have a more positive attitude to communism, at least as a theory, than those of any generation before them. As Christians, both Protestant and Catholic, become more aware of serious social injustices in our nation, some Marxists are looking to build support among Christians more than at any time since the 1930s. For example, the Marxist philosopher Roland Boer recently wrote an essay appealing to Christians, "Why I Am a Christian Communist."[1] The websites of the Communist Party in the United States and the Communist Party of China have been arguing with some vigor recently that Christianity and communism are so compatible that Christians have "nothing to fear" from communists. Given the witness of history and current events, this is a bold and dangerous lie. Churches and believers in Russia and Eastern Europe suffered greatly under communist rule, many Christians in China and Cuba are still under considerable government pressure, and Christians in North Korea are suffering terribly, with regular imprisonment and death. The gospel of Jesus Christ, when preached and enacted as fully as it can be in society, is the answer to communism's atheism, class hatred, and violence. Those Christians who might be attracted to communist ideals should remember that the symbol of Christianity is the cross of Jesus Christ, not a clenched fist.

QUESTIONS FOR REFLECTION AND DISCUSSION

1. Why, in your understanding, does the early Jerusalem church set up a system of sharing like this?
2. How does this "financial oneness" relate to the spiritual and social oneness of the earliest church?
3. Read the positive story of Barnabas, and the sobering story of Ananias and Sapphira (Acts 4:36—5:11). How do these two stories illustrate what Acts is saying about sharing of possessions?

---

1. Boer, "Why I Am a Christian Communist."

4. What does this practice of sharing say about the responsibility of well-off members of the church to others today?

5. What might be some of the reasons why this practice did not continue in the first-century church?

6. What do you think about the first-century church's limitation of its charity to other Christians? What are the pluses and minuses of this for today?

20

How Do All Things Work Together for Good?

We know that all things work together for good for those who love God. (Romans 8:28, RSV)

MANY IMPORTANT PARTS OF life are uncertain. We don't know how long we will live, how healthy we might be in the future, or whether we will prosper materially or not. We don't know how long our friendships might endure. We don't know how our children and grandchildren, if we have them, will fare in life. We do know that some difficulties and disappointments come to every person, and at times several come at once. As William Shakespeare wrote in *Hamlet*, "When sorrows come, they come not [as] single spies, but in battalions." Even people of strong faith can be overwhelmed by the difficulties and sorrows of life.

In his Letter to the Romans, the apostle Paul urges his readers to understand that "All things work together for good for those who love God" (Romans 8:28). This verse is commonly misunderstood to mean that all things in our lives work to our good if we love God. Some Christians take an implication from this that gets to the heart of the misunderstanding: for Christians things naturally have a way of working out for the best in their lives. For Christians who fasten on this verse, this is a powerful but mistaken thought.

This misunderstanding—that things typically work out for our good on their own—is also reflected in popular culture outside the Christian faith. A sign in a popular restaurant in the town where I live says, "Everything will be all right in the end; if it's not all right, it's not the end." The sign says that the author of this saying is unknown, but in reality it is the long title of a 1998 novel by the Brazilian writer Fernando Sabino. This saying has also been wrongly attributed to the late John Lennon and others. It gained more exposure when it figured in the 2012 film *The Best Exotic Marigold Hotel*. At its best, this saying promotes optimism to keep people going in the face of difficulties. It means, "Hang in there, because things will get better." At its worst, it naïvely assumes that things have a way of working out for the best for every individual, if we just wait long enough. This wasn't true in the film, where everything wasn't "all right" for all the main characters in the end. Now this saying, a version of a misunderstood Romans 8:28, can be found on signs, prints, and jewelry.

A few of the Bible's misunderstood verses have uncertain wording in their original language, and Romans 8:28 is one. The traditional translation, "All things work together for good for those who love God," is found in the King James Version (KJV, 1611) and in the two main twentieth-century translations, the Revised Standard Version (RSV) and the New Revised Standard Version (NRSV). Most people who have memorized this verse know it in this form, and this form has enabled the misunderstanding to take root and grow. The uncertain wording of the ancient manuscripts is reflected in the footnotes of most versions of recent times. A footnote to the NRSV says that some manuscripts read "God makes all things work together for good for those who love him," or "in all things God works for good for those who love him." The New International Version (NIV) reads, "We know that in all things God works for the good of those who love him," but then says in a footnote that some manuscripts read, "We know that all things work together for good to those who love God."[1]

Why does this uncertainty arise in the wording? The issue of correctly understanding this sentence was evidently felt as a problem by the Christian scribes who copied this verse in the second, third, and fourth centuries. By

---

1. The New Testament's wording in the manuscripts is rarely so uncertain that the meaning of a verse is affected. This is bit more of a problem in the Old Testament, because our knowledge of biblical Hebrew is not as full as our knowledge of ancient Greek, but even in the Old Testament it doesn't affect more than a very small proportion of passages. This rare uncertainty about wording is one of the results of having God's word in human words.

adding the word "God," they were attempting to solve a problem connected to the modern misunderstanding of this verse: do things work for good on their own, or does God work in them to make them good? Most biblical scholars conclude that the traditional wording, without the addition of "God" (before "works together," right before "is") is probably the original wording that Paul wrote. This is because it is much more likely that a few scribes would add "God" to this sentence than it is that most scribes would omit "God." The New Testament was copied only by committed Christians, who would not leave God out of the picture in this passage.

Whatever the original wording, this much-loved verse testifies *in its context* to God's sovereign control over life, and care for the lives of believers. It does not mean in its context that "things have a way of turning out for the best." This is the gospel according to Pollyanna, not the gospel of Jesus Christ. Romans 8:28 doesn't promise that we will land a better job if we lose a good job, or sell our house at a surprisingly good profit if circumstances force us to sell it. Paul nowhere says anything like that, because he knows that God guides life. Human events do not guide themselves to God-approved results in the present age, because human life in this age is turned away from God. Things turn out the way that God wants them to turn out, and believers can gain confidence in this.

How do we know that the corrected understanding is indeed right? First, the order of the Greek words suggests it. The verse literally runs, "We know that to those who love God all things work together for good, to those who are called according to [God's] purpose." Notice that the strong parallel of "to those who love God" and "to those who are called" by God, with "all things work together for good" sandwiched firmly between them. This wording suggests that God's calling and God's purpose for us enable us to see God working in all things.

A second way to know that this meaning is indeed correct is to look at what immediately precedes it, and how this context shapes this verse. In Romans 8:26–27, Paul writes lyrically about how the Spirit of God in believers intercedes with God for believers when they don't know how to pray. In moments of great weakness, when we don't even know how to pray (vv. 26–27), we can be confident that God is working in all the circumstances of our lives to bring about our good (v. 28). This makes prayer more confident and faithful, even if it remains difficult.

What does the misunderstanding get right about this verse? First, it usually acknowledges that God is in the picture when all things work for good: "to those who love God." Many Christians probably are not naïve enough to suppose that things work on their own for good. Next, the misunderstanding knows that God actively cares for his people and guides the events of their lives for their good and God's glory. They know there is great spiritual power in this verse.

What are the implications of the corrected understanding of this verse for us today? The first implication can be seen in the context of Romans 8:28. Paul says that Jesus came to save both Jews and Gentiles from death, and this creates a new human family. This family will share in the re-creation of the world, when "creation itself will be liberated from its bondage to decay" (v. 21). The promise in Romans 8:28 is not just for any good outcome, like finding a great new job or selling a house for more than the asking price. It's more than just a "happy ending" for us; it is a blessed ending for the whole universe, the renewal of all things. The world is still groaning, and we groan with it. But God's Spirit is with us in our groaning, and will bring it out for good. That's what Romans 8:28 says.

A second takeaway for us from the correct meaning of this verse puts it in the context of Paul's whole body of letters. Paul's basic Christian perspectives are shaped by Scripture and by the death and resurrection of Jesus, and Paul's view of life is God-centered. Scripture is full of examples of how God guides all things in life, both good and evil, for his own purposes. Joseph was sold into slavery by his brothers, but God used it to bring Joseph to great power in Egypt and preserve his kin in times of famine. He tells his brothers, "You meant it for evil, but God meant it for good" (Genesis 50:20). Naomi and Ruth go through all sorts of suffering, but God guides their lives to bring marriage for Ruth and Boaz, a marriage that eventually produces King David and eventually Jesus himself. The most important example of God turning all things into good is in the death and resurrection of Jesus: God brings life out of death, victory from defeat, hope from despair, and a new age out of the present age. The enemies of Jesus did something monstrously evil, but God turned it into something so good that it surpasses our ability to understand or even imagine its goodness.

Moreover, the apostle Paul had a strong belief in divine providence, particularly the belief that God is a master at turning evil into good, for the human race as a whole and for each individual person. This came not only from his background as a Pharisee, but especially from his understanding of how God has acted in the death and resurrection of Jesus Christ. Paul would not mean something like "things have a way of working out,"

How Do All Things Work Together for Good?

because he knows that this is a fallen world where bad things, when left on their own, generally go from bad to worse. If all things in this world had to work out on their own, Joseph would have perished as a slave in Egypt, Ruth would have died childless, and Jesus (perish the thought!) would still be dead. But those who believe in God's power and sovereignty know that God is working all things together for good in their lives.

Here is a final takeaway. Paul gives a reason ("for") the truth of v. 28: "For those whom [God] foreknew, he also predestined to become conformed to the image of his Son" (Romans 8:29). When troubles assail us, God seems to have a different good for us than quickly ending our troubles in this life when we ask for this. (This can happen, but evidently it is not God's purpose for most people.) Christians trust that God uses every disappointment, difficulty and hardship to make us more like Jesus: in Paul's words, through hardship we are "conformed to the image of [God's] Son." Perhaps you must remain single, like Jesus. Perhaps you must live in humble circumstances, like Jesus. Perhaps you suffer unfairly, and the good that you do is misunderstood by others around you, like Jesus. Whatever our difficulties and challenges may be, God's promise is that none of it is wasted, because God guides our lives. The path of our salvation is certain and complete. It stretches from before we were born ("foreknew... predestined") through all our life to our death and our going to be with Christ in heaven until the end of this world, and finally to our gaining full life in our bodily resurrection at the re-creation of the world, when we will live forever in a new heaven and a new earth. All things on this path do work for good because God is walking with us. That is as good as "all things" can get for us—becoming like Jesus more and more in this life, and being transformed in the resurrection to his full image.

QUESTIONS FOR REFLECTION AND DISCUSSION

1. What do you think about the idea that eventually everything naturally works out for each individual's good? Is this a common idea in our culture? Why or why not?

2. What is the more careful understanding of this verse, and what does that imply? Why does it matter?

3. When Paul says that all things work for "good", what does "good" mean?

4. Reflect on this statement: "Faith is not about having everything turn out okay, but being okay with however things turn out."

5. What hope does this verse offer? Do you sense this hope in yourself? How so?

6. How does Bible translation affect the understanding of Scripture? Of this verse? How do we know what translation to rely on?

7. Can you think of an example of a time when God turned something bad into something good? In the Bible? In our day?

21

Will God Give Us More Than We Can Bear?

God is faithful, and he will not let you be tested beyond your strength. (1 Corinthians 10:13)

"GOD NEVER GIVES US more than we can bear." This saying, meant to offer comfort and hope, is used in a variety of settings. It is said by people in distress: in deep grief after the death of a loved one, after a messy divorce, in anxiety over the loss of a job, in worry over a sick child, in uncertainty during a spiritual crisis. People going through difficulties like this are told, "Things will be all right, because God wouldn't give you this trouble if you couldn't handle it." This assurance is usually spoken with emphatic certainty, because it is thought to be a quotation from 1 Corinthians 10:13: "God is faithful, and he will not let you be tested beyond your strength." This verse does seem to have great power to assure Christians that they will come through their trials.

However, to other Christians this use of 1 Corinthians 10:13 does not seem to match up with Scripture or their everyday experience of the Christian life. One of them told me that "God will not give you more than you can bear" is hardly better than a fortune-cookie saying, and unworthy of use by serious Christians. This is probably too harsh, but it does raise the question: Is this verse used correctly by those who think it means "God will never give you more than you can bear"?

To answer this question, we should start by reading this verse in its context. The Corinthian church had many problems, which Paul deals with one by one in 1 Corinthians. In 10:1–5, the apostle warns the Corinthians against a variety of sins. He is especially concerned about the sin of idolatry, serving other gods in addition to the one true God (whether an idol is used or not). Some Corinthians are confusing buying meat offered to idols, which Paul permits under certain conditions, and participating in the worship of these idols, which he forbids. He recounts that the people of Israel had miraculous experiences in being delivered from Egypt and living in the wilderness before entering the promised land, but they still followed other gods when they worshiped the golden calf at the foot of Mount Sinai. God punished them severely for these sins. Many died immediately in their punishment. Paul continues,

> 6 Now these things occurred as examples for us, so that we might not desire evil as they did. 7 Do not become idolaters as some of them did; as it is written, "The people sat down to eat and drink, and they rose up to play." 8 We must not indulge in sexual immorality as some of them did, and twenty-three thousand fell in a single day. 9 We must not put Christ to the test, as some of them did, and were destroyed by serpents. 10 And do not complain as some of them did, and were destroyed by the destroyer. 11 These things happened to them to serve as an example, and they were written down to instruct us, on whom the ends of the ages have come. 12 So if you think you are standing, watch out that you do not fall. 13 No testing [or "temptation"] has overtaken you that is not common to everyone. God is faithful, and he will not let you be tested [or "tempted"] beyond your strength, but with the testing [or "temptation"] he will also provide the way out so that you may be able to endure it.

Paul continues in verse 14 by returning to his main point, that the Corinthians must "flee from the worship of idols."

Now let's take a closer look at this passage. After recounting the several ways that the people of Israel sinned in the wilderness and were severely punished for it, Paul says twice that these things are "examples" of behavior to avoid; they "were written down to instruct us," Christians who are living at the dawn of the new age (v. 11). The implication is that God still punishes sin in severe ways. Paul warns them, "If you think you are standing [strong and faithful, like the Israelites thought of themselves], watch out that you do not fall [into sin, as they did]." This is a real possibility, Paul says, and he implies that the sins of Israel described in vv. 6–10 are going on among the Corinthian believers today. Then comes the immediate context of our misunderstood verse: "No testing [temptation] has overtaken you that is not common to everyone" (v. 13). Paul assures them here that they are not facing anything unusual that the people of God have not always faced. Finally, he says in the culmination of this paragraph, "God is faithful, and he will not let you be tested [tempted] beyond your strength, but with the testing [temptation] he will also provide the way out so that you may be able to endure it" (v. 13).

The first thing to say about this misunderstood verse deals with its translation. Is that key word "testing" or "temptation"? The Greek word underneath it can be translated in these two ways, closely related but each with a different nuance. Many contemporary English versions (including the NRSV, quoted above) address this issue in a footnote; the alternate translation is given above in brackets. "Testing" is the wider concept, covering all sorts of trials that may or may not involve the possibility of falling into sin, such as personal difficulties in life. "Temptation" is the narrower concept, always meaning a trial that involves the possibility of falling into sin. Obviously, the distinction between them is not complete, because certain kinds of personal testing can lead not only to loss of faith but to loss of obedience to God as well; this gets close to what "temptation" is. Nevertheless, there is a difference between "testing" and "temptation," and it figures in the misunderstanding of this verse.

If both "trials" and "temptations" could fit this verse, how can we decide which is better? The context shows the way forward. Is 1 Corinthians 10 speaking about tests of our faith that are "trials," or about enticements to sin that are "temptations"? This whole chapter is clearly about temptation to sin. Israel sinned in the wilderness, and the Corinthians are threatened with serious sin now. The Corinthians, in their spiritual pride, think they are "standing" strong in the faith, but Paul warns them that they may soon "fall" (v. 12); this is the language of temptation and sin. The good news that Paul then shares with them is twofold. First, he assures them that all the temptations to sin that they face are common temptations for the people of God, implying that the Corinthians can deal with them. The Israelites fell into sin so deeply that they could not recover, but the Corinthians need not do so. Second, Paul says that God is faithful, in this way: temptation may threaten to overwhelm the believer, but God provides a way to endure (we might say "cope with") temptation. Temptations will come, but God provides strength to escape them without falling into destruction as the ancient Israelites did. So the better way to translate this word is "temptations." This is why current English translations (with the notable exception of the NRSV) say "tempt," with a footnote giving "test."

What is being promised in this verse, after so many dire warnings against sin? This important and empowering point: God will not let us be trapped in sin so fully that we cannot repent and be restored. In other words, God will hold on to us even when our hold on God begins to fail. Paul has already told the Corinthians in the beginning of this letter that "[God] will sustain you to the end, guiltless on the day of Christ" (1 Corinthians 1:8). He wrote to the Philippians (1:6), "I am confident that [God] who began a good work in you will bring it to completion by the day of Jesus Christ." 1 Peter 1:5 has this same thought, "[you] are being protected by the power of God through faith for a salvation ready to be revealed in the last time."

Other passages in the New Testament show that this popular understanding of 1 Corinthians 10:13, that "God never gives us trials we can't handle," is not correct. (Here we put aside for a moment the fact that temptation is really in view in this verse, and look at the validity of "trials.") Sometimes God does give us heavy burdens that seem to break us or in fact do break us in certain ways. We begin with Paul himself, who spoke of his difficulties: "We do not want you to be unaware, brothers and sisters, of the affliction we experienced in Asia; for we were so utterly, unbearably crushed that we despaired of life itself" (2 Corinthians 1:8). This is almost the opposite of Paul saying "God didn't give us anything we couldn't cope with in Asia." Throughout Scripture, we see good, faithful people overpowered by what happens to them. This even applies to Jesus, too, who dies in agony on the cross, crying out, "My God, My God, why have you forsaken me?" (Mark 15:34, Matthew 27:46). But none of these troubles caused those who suffered them to fall away completely from God. Even the laments or complaints these verses give voice to are the words of people who know that God is holding on to them. In modern life as well, Christians suffer great hardships; war, famine, poverty, and chronic sickness come to them. God is still faithful, and even though our grip on God may fail, God never lets go of us. But God doesn't only hold on to us; God directs us in his way and holds us in it, and we are responsible to walk in it.

What is the significance of the corrected understanding of this verse? First, temptations will indeed come our way. No version of the Christian life prevents all temptation. God allows temptation to come to us in order to strengthen our faith and increase our dependence on his grace. Besides, if Jesus was tempted to sin by God's design (the Spirit drove him into the wilderness to be tempted by Satan, the gospels say), it is certain that we will be tempted as well. Not only temptations to sin will come, but personal trials of faith will come as well. In the Psalms we read words that sound like 2 Corinthians 1:8, "I am utterly spent and crushed; I groan because of the tumult of my heart" (Psalm 38:8). But the psalmist knows, as Paul does, that this is the lament of one who knows that God cares for us in the midst of all our difficulties.

Here is a second takeaway: trials will come to us, too. When people say, "God never gives you more than you can handle," do they mean that we will never fail a test or trial that God sends us? The Bible offers no support for an idea like that. Peter sank into the waves, and much more seriously, denied Jesus. If we had perfect faith in Christ, we might come through every test and trial successfully. But God does not give us that kind of perfection. We can conclude that God will indeed never give us more than we can handle, but only if we mean God will sustain us though temptations and trials that threaten our relationship with God. God provides "the way out" of both trial and temptation; we don't find our own way out of it.

Third, this verse says that it is by God's presence and power that we can bear temptation. When Paul says, "God won't give what is beyond what you are able" (v. 12), he means, "Not beyond what you are able with God's help." We know this because he says next, "with the tempting [God] will also provide the way out so that you may be able to endure it." Because God is faithful to us, God also protects us in all the difficult things he sends our way. In the words of the Lord's Prayer, we ask God to "deliver us from evil," and we trust that God will. We must depend on this protection, and look for the "way out" of temptation, which God provides.

QUESTIONS FOR REFLECTION AND DISCUSSION

1. Is it correct to say that "all temptation is testing, but not all testing is temptation"?
2. Can you identify in your own life times of testing that differ from times of temptation? If you are willing to do so and think it wise, share this experience with others.

3. Some Protestants believe that God's people will persevere as Christians to the end—in other words, "Once saved, always saved." Others believe that salvation can be lost. What does this passage suggest?

4. How is saying, "God will enable us to handle temptations" different from saying that *nothing* will happen to us that we cannot handle?

5. Reflect on this observation, taking into account all the problems in 1 Corinthians: We sometimes think the New Testament church was ideal, and that we should be more like so-called New Testament Christians, but the truth is that we are already too much like them!

6. What is the comfort offered by the corrected understanding of this verse?

22

What Things Can I Do in Christ?

I can do all things through him who strengthens me. (Philippians 4:13)

IN THE FINAL GAME of the 1990 NCAA Division III women's basketball tournament, a Hope College player put her team over the top with two free throws. "We never gave up. We kept the faith," she said to the press after she calmly gave Hope a stunning win. When asked how she stayed cool under so much pressure, she said that she repeated to herself at the free-throw line, "I can do all things through Christ who strengthens me." Most Christians appreciated her faith, and her willingness to speak about it. It's good to see Christians steady their mind on Jesus. After all, they could use other mental activities to calm their minds and steady their hands.

The Christian faith does indeed encourage us to rely on God to live a faithful life, and a measure of fulfillment and joy will come to us. Philippians 4:13 is echoed in the New Testament—for example in Matthew 19:26: "With God all things are possible," or in the challenge from Mark 11:23 to followers of Jesus to have a faith that can "move mountains." These verses and others like them have been the favorites of power-of-positive-thinking preachers from Norman Vincent Peale in the 1950s to Robert Schuller in the last generation and now to Joel Osteen. Prosperity gospel preachers, who proclaim that salvation brings physical health and material prosperity, also fasten on this verse. But these preachers, sports figures, and many ordinary Christians often understand "I can do all things" to mean something along these lines: "I can do anything I desire if I really believe. I can land this job, get that promotion, win this game, or pass that test." As we will see, this kind of thinking seriously distorts Philippians 4:13.

This verse is lifted out of context and applied to a whole variety of things that Scripture doesn't have in view. Many items of commercial jewelry now feature this verse. It is especially popular among Christian athletes as a motivational saying. It is emblazoned on basketballs, baseballs, and footballs. (You can find many examples online.) It is written on locker-room doors at several Christian colleges to inspire athletes as they move onto the fields or courts for their games. In short, because "all things" is such a general expression and can be applied to almost anything, this Bible verse has become the favorite for those seeking greater self-confidence and achievement in life.

Why does Paul say that he can do all things through Christ, and imply that other believers can do the same? When we look at the whole meaning of this verse in context, we see clearly what Paul means by "all things." Here is the passage that forms the context for Philippians 4:13:

> 10 I rejoice in the Lord greatly that now at length you have revived your concern for me; you were indeed concerned for me, but you had no opportunity. 11 Not that I complain of want; for I have learned, in whatever state I am, to be content. 12 I know how to be abased, and I know how to abound; in any and all circumstances I have learned the secret of facing plenty and hunger, abundance and want. 13 I can do all things in him who strengthens me. 14 Yet it was kind of you to share my trouble. (RSV)

Paul is clearly talking about "doing all things" to endure the troubles of the Christian life, especially the troubles of his missionary calling that he talks about in the verses immediately before and after this one. He is not speaking of the ordinary troubles of life. Philippians 4:13 should be understood not as "I can *do* all things" but as "I can *endure* all things." When Paul's affirmation that Christ empowers him to endure all the trials that come his way becomes "Christ empowers me to do whatever I set my mind to," Christ can be reduced to a motivational tool. It should be enough for us, as it was for Paul, to endure all the challenges that come our way because we follow the hard way of Christ. Greco-Roman culture was sports obsessed, almost as much as North American culture is today, but Paul would not have thought that "I can do all things through Christ" applies to success in sports or to making a good living or any other ordinary or extraordinary personal goal in life. Paul means that we can do everything *God* wants, but not everything *we* want.

The current edition of the New International Version of the Bible wisely suggests the correct meaning of this verse. Instead of rendering it "I can do all things," it says "I can do all this," which obviously refers back to Paul's missionary hardships. This is indirect as a translation, but it is an accurate statement of the contextual meaning of this verse. It gives a specific reference to the general Greek word "all," which implies only "things" by its grammatical form. The "all things" we can do are enduring the hardships we encounter as Christians. It is ironic that the "do all things" phrase so often misunderstood to teach "in Christ you can do or have all things you want" is found in a context where Paul says he can endure all sorts of deprivation and hardship.

Someone might ask, what's the harm in this misunderstanding? What's so wrong with giving Christians a strong faith in their potential? The harm is this: If we can't do the things we want, things that we have set our hearts on Christ to give us power to do, then we may have a crisis of faith. What if things don't work out the way we want? What if we don't get into that selective college, land a certain job, or become a professional athlete, no matter how much we believe and how much we try? Failure might call into question for us the goodness of God or even God's love for us. Some people have left the faith because of this bitter experience. Or they judge themselves to be bad Christians and become discouraged because they didn't believe enough. Even the apostle Paul couldn't do "all things" he wanted. Paul could not get out of the prison where he wrote this letter to the Philippians, no matter how intensely he believed in Jesus. He was there until God let him go, and Paul recognized the possibility that he might be sentenced to death and never leave prison alive (Philippians 1:12–26, 2:17–18). Being a person in Christ was more important to him than getting out of prison, and this strengthened him to be content. This contentment in turn gave him a confidence in the future, and it made most other Christians more bold in speaking the gospel (1:14).

A helpful example of Paul's learning to be content when things didn't go his way concerns his "thorn in the flesh," which he writes about in 2 Corinthians 12:7b–10. We don't know what this was, but it certainly was serious to Paul:

> 7 And to keep me from being too elated by the abundance of revelations, a thorn was given me in the flesh, a messenger of Satan.

... ⁸ Three times I besought the Lord about this, that it should leave me; ⁹ but he said to me, "My grace is sufficient for you, for my power is made perfect in weakness." I will all the more gladly boast of my weaknesses, that the power of Christ may rest upon me. ¹⁰ For the sake of Christ, then, I am content with weaknesses, insults, hardships, persecutions, and calamities; for when I am weak, then I am strong. (RSV)

Paul could do or endure "all things in Christ," but this did not mean that his prayers for healing were answered. Instead, it meant that he became content to bear this weakness, because this follows the example of Jesus, who became weak and died for us. Note that Paul expands his list of difficulties from illness to other items: "weakness, insults, distresses, persecutions, and calamities." Becoming content with weaknesses and setbacks, and learning to accept God's no to our prayers, is life conformed to the cross, not to the crown.

What might those who misunderstand this verse get right about it? First, they do see the positive message Paul wants to convey in this verse. Even though Christians can be surrounded by many difficulties and challenges, they can trust that there is a way out of them. Second, they know that it is Christ who empowers them. When they quote this verse, they always remember to quote "through him who strengthens me," and they know that "him" is Christ. They don't think that this strength comes from within ourselves, as if all we had to do is concentrate our own thoughts and wills in order to accomplish "all things."

One takeaway from the corrected understanding of this verse deals with how we raise children. Sometimes we tell our children to encourage them, "You can be anything you want" and, leaning on this verse's "do all things," we expect that God will strengthen them through Christ to make this happen. But this expectation when taken too literally misinterprets God's word, and raises unrealistic expectations. Common sense and our experience of life tell us that all things are not in fact achievable. If one can't learn the natural sciences at a high academic level, one won't be a physician no matter how much one believes. If one is blind, becoming a commercial airline pilot is out of the question. And consider a young man I know of who wants to make a career as a professional basketball player. He's modestly gifted as an athlete, with an above-average (but not excellent) record in small-college basketball. In short, he's not National Basketball Association (NBA) material. But he is convinced that God is calling him to play in the NBA and be a Christian witness there, and he claims this verse as his own. He practices or plays basketball for hours every day, and as a result, he is not doing as well in his studies as he could. He is headed for a rude awakening when he leaves college unable to enter the NBA and unprepared for work.

Another takeaway from an accurate understanding of Philippians 4:13 is this: We can "do all things" by living a contented and effective Christian life no matter what our circumstances. When our obedience to the gospel brings us into various difficulties and threats, this verse is appropriately applied to our situation. We can "do all things" God wants us to do because Jesus has done, and is doing, all things necessary for our salvation.

QUESTIONS FOR REFLECTION AND DISCUSSION

1. Prior to this study, how did you think about Philippians 4:13?
2. Have you noticed this verse being used in our culture? If so, how?
3. How might telling our children, "You can be anything you want to be" be more reflective of the American Dream than it is of the gospel?
4. How does our perspective on this verse change if we think of it, not so much as saying "*do* all things," but rather as saying "*endure* all things"?
5. How can we avoid using Christ as a motivational tool? Why is this important?
6. Have you ever had a circumstance that made you question God's goodness or even God's existence because you had gotten the idea that being a Christian and having faith means we can do anything? If not, have you known someone like that?

23

What Is the Root of All Evil?

For the love of money is the root of all evil. (1 Timothy 6:10)

BIBLE VERSES ARE SOMETIMES misunderstood because they are misquoted, and one way to misquote them is to omit key words. A prominent example is this familiar statement drawn from the King James Version, "Money is the root of all evil." First Timothy 6:10 is so commonly quoted this way that we may wonder if many people at all know its full, correct form, "The love of money is the root of all evil." The shortened "Money is the root of all evil" has reached the status of a modern proverb. One hears it applied to politics, the idea that money has a corrupting influence in government. One hears it when corporations go astray in seeking to maximize their profits, as when one of the largest banks in America was charged in 2016 with committing massive fraud for years against its own customers. Football fans may have heard that the controversial former quarterback of the San Francisco 49ers, Colin Kaepernick, got a tattoo on his torso that reads, "Money is the root of all evil." The tattoo features images combining Genesis 3 and this verse: an arm encircled by a snake is holding up an apple, and above and below the arm are piles of cash.

People who misunderstand this verse come close to quoting 1 Timothy 6:10 correctly, but omitting "the love of" makes a significant difference. "Money is the root of all evil" implies that money itself, the physical object, is an evil thing. It also implies that money always produces evil. Some Christians today speak of money as "filthy lucre," a phrase with a biblical origin (1 Timothy 3:3, 8; Titus 1:7, 11; 1 Peter 5:2—all in the KJV). That phrase may be declining in use, but it survives in our common expression "filthy rich." If it were true that money itself is filthy, all our possession and use of money would be evil. This is not what Titus 1:11 means; "filthy lucre" is connected in 1 Timothy and Titus with ill-gotten gains by false teachers in the church.

Let's look now more closely at the full quotation of 1 Timothy 6:10 in its context, and how the context makes clear that "*the love of* money is the root of all evil." First Timothy as a whole shows a notable concern for money, its uses and abuses. In 1 Timothy 2:9 wealthy Christian women are urged to dress modestly, not richly. In the ancient Roman world, as in much of the world today, women more than men displayed the wealth of their family by their clothing, jewelry, and hairstyles. In 3:3, in a list of qualifications for the office of bishop, the bishop must not be "a lover of money," and likewise in 3:8 deacons must not be "greedy for money." In 5:3–8, the letter stresses the duty to provide monetarily for widowed relatives. First Timothy 5:17–18 commands a "double honor" for elders who rule well.

In 1 Timothy 6:3, the author picks up again another theme of this letter: rejection of false teaching and false teachers. He levels several charges against false teachers: that they are conceited, do not comprehend the faith, have a morbid love of controversies, and have other moral faults that come from these (vv. 3–5a). Those who spread false teaching "think that godliness is a means to financial gain" (1 Timothy 6:5). The author continues at some length on this theme:

> 6 But godliness with contentment is great gain. 7 For we brought nothing into the world, and we can take nothing out of it. 8 But if we have food and clothing, we will be content with that. 9 Those who want to get rich fall into temptation and a trap and into many foolish and harmful desires that plunge people into ruin and destruction. 10 For the love of money is a root of all kinds of evil. Some people, eager for money, have wandered from the faith and pierced themselves with many griefs. (NIV)

Near the end of 1 Timothy, a letter with a main goal of refuting false teaching that threatens the church, the false teachers come into view. After saying that they "think that godliness is a means of gain," implying that they lead the church to enrich themselves (v. 5), the author reverses the idea of "gain": "There is great gain in godliness combined with contentment" (v. 6). He then alludes to a scriptural proverb from Job 1:21: "We brought nothing into the world, so we can take nothing out of it" (v. 7). He applies it to the value of living with the necessities of life: "But if we have food and clothing, we will be content with that" (v. 8). The opposite of this contentment is a desire for wealth, a dangerous thing: "Those who want to get rich fall into temptation and a trap and into many foolish and harmful desires that plunge people into ruin and destruction" (v. 9) Then comes our verse: "For the love of money is a root of all kinds of evil. Some people, eager for money, have wandered from the faith and pierced themselves with many griefs" (v. 10).

Now we must take a closer look at the wording of this verse. It begins with "For," a little word that should not be overlooked, because it indicates that this sentence (v. 10) gives the reason behind the sentence before it (v. 9). (As biblical interpreters like to say, "When you see a 'for' there, you should always ask what it's there for.") The "love of money" phrase may seem a bit unclear to us—what exactly does it entail? The passage explains this in the next sentence: it is a desire to be rich. Although the King James Version says that the love of money is "*the* root of all evil" (which appears in the misquotation), almost all more recent translations say "*a* root of all evil," because the word "the" is notably absent in the Greek original. Evil has other roots beside the love of money. Also in that expression, "all evil" is better translated as many modern versions render it, as "all kinds of evil." These different kinds of evil have already been indicated in 1 Timothy 1:9–10; 3:3, 8; and 6:4–5. But the theme continues in the rest of v. 10: "Some people, eager for money, have wandered from the faith and pierced themselves with many griefs." The love of money is a root of doctrinal and moral error that leads to many self-inflicted wounds.

Later in this chapter vv. 17–19 continue this theme, and are an important part of the context for our misunderstood verse. The author returns in v. 17 to the theme of rich Christians, which shows how important this topic is to him. "As for those who in the present age are rich, command them not to be haughty" (v. 17). In the ancient world as well as today, the rich can think of themselves as better than others. This leads to spiritual pride and a host of other faults. The author implies that those who are rich "in the present age" (v. 17a) may not enjoy riches in the coming age of God's kingdom. This idea is found in Jesus' teaching on the great reversal in the kingdom of God (Luke 1:51–53; 6:20–23; 13:30). The rich won't have their riches forever, so they should make good use of them in the present. Wealthy believers are to turn away their hopes from "the uncertainty of riches" (v.

17b). A more literal translation of this brings out the meaning better: "on riches, which are uncertain." Turning one's hope away from possessions can be done by setting hope on God, "who richly provides us with everything for our enjoyment." If well-to-do Christians are "generous and willing to share," they "store up real treasure for the future," and live now and in the future "the life that really is life" (v. 19).

What do people who misunderstand this verse have correct? To grant them the benefit of a doubt, people who say "Money is the root of all evil" often take "money" to mean attachment to money, greed, covetousness, or something similar. They correctly warn against this kind of attachment to money and the things it can buy. This is getting closer to the real meaning of 1 Timothy 6:10. But this misquotation still does damage. It implies that physical things can be evil in themselves, which is not at all a biblical idea. It also promotes an unbiblical and extreme attitude to money—that it's all "filthy lucre," no matter how much of it we have, and no matter how we gain it or use it. This negative attitude runs against the main biblical statements about money and possessions, and in particular it directly contradicts what is said in 1 Timothy 6:17–19.

What are the implications of this corrected understanding for today? First, contrary to a saying popular in the 1980s and that is making a comeback in some circles today, "Greed is good," this passage states that greed is not good. (First Timothy uses the expression "love of money," a close synonym to "greed.") Saying "greed is good" to secure a better financial future is the equivalent of saying "lust is good" to promote love between a husband and wife, something also heard occasionally today. We should never expect that one of the traditional seven deadly sins can bring life. Greed can only diminish what God intends for human life.

The second takeaway from a corrected understanding of 1 Timothy 6:10 is the theme of contentment that runs through the surrounding verses. Being content with the basics of life runs counter to strong currents in our North American culture: get as wealthy as you can, buy as much as you want, and enjoy it as much as you can. Contentment is the opposite of covetousness and the consumerism that feeds it. The Greek word for both "covetousness" and "greed," *pleonexia* [pronounced pleh-on-ek-SEE-ah], is constructed from word elements for "have-more-ness." Money and possessions can be addicting; we need to have more of them all the time because their "high," like a dangerous drug, wears off. This can be countered only by faith in God's provision of all that we need. We should learn to be content with what God provides, as challenging as this might be; only this contentment brings happiness and spiritual maturity.

Third, the context of this verse in 1 Timothy raises the perennial question of money and church leaders. The presence of church leaders who use their roles to enrich themselves (or who, in the words of 1 Timothy 6:5, see "godliness [as] a means of gain") seems to be a permanent problem. Pope Francis, who lives simply and frugally compared to most previous popes, has urged those Roman Catholic bishops who live affluently in immodest church-owned residences to stop doing so. A few times he has ordered some bishops to move to modest quarters. Health-and-wealth preachers want to live ostentatiously in great wealth gained from their ministries, in part as a demonstration to others that the health-and-wealth gospel really does work. Although very few Christians enter the rank-and-file ministry in Protestant churches for its pay and benefits, they still must guard carefully their feelings and attitudes about their compensation. Even for them, "be content with what you have" is a spiritual challenge.

QUESTIONS FOR REFLECTION AND DISCUSSION

1. A common complaint against the church today is that its leaders use religion to get money from church members. How accurate or important do you think this complaint is?

2. What do you think of the statement, "You can't take it with you, but you can send it on ahead"? How might this relate to 1 Timothy 6:7, 19?

3. How do we know if we "love money" and have an "eagerness to be rich"?

4. Jesus taught his disciples, "You cannot serve God and wealth" (Matthew 6:24; Luke 16:13). What does this have to contribute to our understanding of the topic of greed?

5. Where do you find the love of money in yourself?

6. What does a good understanding of this verse have to say to the prosperity gospel (see chapter 5, above)?

24

Why Is Jesus Knocking at the Door?

Behold, I stand at the door and knock. If anyone hears my voice and opens the door, I will come in to him and eat with him, and he with me. (Revelation 3:20)

THE IMAGE OF JESUS standing at the door and knocking for entrance is powerful and meaningful to many people. Several artists in Germany and Great Britain during the 1800s painted this scene from Revelation 3:20, and their paintings were commonly reproduced in prints. The most significant painting of this sort, *The Light of the World*, was done in 1854 by William Holman Hunt. Hunt shows Jesus, lantern in hand and wearing both a crown of thorns and a crown of glory. He is knocking on a long-unopened door overgrown with weeds. The outside of the door has no handle, and can therefore be opened only from the inside. Ancient doors generally had no openings to see out, because this would greatly diminish their security. Hunt put an opening at eye level to suggest that the person behind the door can see Jesus outside and hear him more easily. He painted Jesus looking directly at the viewer of the painting, implying that Jesus is knocking for this viewer. In case some still didn't get the point of the painting, Hunt painted the words of Revelation 3:20 at the bottom of the canvas, an unusual thing to do in a painting of a biblical scene. Hunt later made a duplicate of this painting, which was given an extensive world tour before it was hung permanently in Saint Paul's Cathedral in London. *The Light of the World* became one of the most widely viewed paintings on earth; when it was in Australia, for example, an estimated 80 percent of all Australians saw it.

Evangelicals in North America generally prefer a similar painting by Warner Sallman, *Christ at Heart's Door*. Painted in the 1940s, it became one of the most reproduced religious artworks of all time, second only to Sallman's *Head of Christ*. It can be found today in many Protestant churches and homes, and photos of it and Hunt's painting can be found online. For most people, Sallman's painting is more inviting to look at and easier to understand than Hunt's, because Sallman simplified Hunt's painting as he borrowed from it. Christ himself seems to glow with a light that illumines the whole foreground. The thorns and thistles of sin can be seen around one side of the door. A small iron-bar opening in the door reveals the darkness within, and Christ seems to be looking through this opening in a direct appeal to the person inside to open the door and let him in.

For many American Christians, these paintings picture their own conversion experiences: they were locked away in their own darkness, and when Christ came knocking on their door, they opened up to him and were saved. Today the predominant interpretation of Revelation 3:20 gives it this evangelical, salvation-related meaning. It's a favorite verse for preachers seeking to bring others to faith: "Jesus is knocking on your door," they say; "Will you let him in?" One sermon said, "As lost people go through life, there is a loving savior who persistently and gently knocks at their heart's door so they can be saved."[1]

Though we should not discount one bit the gospel's call for people to experience the invitation of Christ and let him in, this interpretation is a misunderstanding of Revelation 3:20. This verse is not really about Christ knocking at heart's door for conversion. A closer look at this verse will make that clear, but first let's look at the whole passage:

> 14 "And to the angel of the church in Laodicea write: The words of the Amen, the faithful and true witness, the origin of God's creation:
>
> 15 "I know your works; you are neither cold nor hot. I wish that you were either cold or hot. 16 So, because you are lukewarm, and neither cold nor hot, I am about to spit you out of my mouth. 17 For you say, 'I am rich, I have prospered, and I need nothing.' You do not realize that you are wretched, pitiable, poor, blind, and naked. 18 Therefore I counsel you to buy from me gold refined by fire so that you may be rich; and white robes to clothe you and to

---

1. Lloyd, "Jesus Is Knocking."

keep the shame of your nakedness from being seen; and salve to anoint your eyes so that you may see. ¹⁹ I reprove and discipline those whom I love. Be earnest, therefore, and repent. ²⁰ Listen! I am standing at the door, knocking; if you hear my voice and open the door, I will come in to you and eat with you, and you with me. ²¹ To the one who conquers I will give a place with me on my throne, just as I myself conquered and sat down with my Father on his throne. ²² Let anyone who has an ear listen to what the Spirit is saying to the churches."

This passage is found in one of the letters to the seven churches of Asia Minor (today, western Turkey) that begin the book of Revelation: the church of Laodicea. Like all the letters that begin Revelation, this one is addressed to people already in a church, not on the outside. Also, it is addressed to the whole church as a group, not to individuals in the church. Jesus has strong words for them. Jesus has found them lukewarm and would soon spit them out of his mouth (3:16). They think they are rich in faith and lacking nothing, but God knows that they are "wretched, pitiable, poor, blind, and naked"; in other words, they are as needy as they can be (v. 17). Christ says to them, "Those whom I love, I reprove and chasten [discipline], so be zealous and repent." Then come the famous words, more well known in this RSV form than in their NRSV form, "Behold, I stand at the door and knock. If anyone hears my voice and opens the door, I will come in to him and eat with him, and he with me" (vv. 19–20). This setting makes it clear that Jesus is not knocking for the conversion of unbelievers; he is knocking for the repentance of his own people. They hear the voice of Jesus and recognize him because they already belong to him. He is calling for them to let him in for deeper, purer fellowship. He will accept their repentance, and eat and drink with them, just as he did with Zacchaeus (Luke 19:1–10) and other repentant members of the people of God. Although this verse seems to talk about individuals ("anyone," "him"), and although individuals in the church have a role in letting Jesus in, it is clear that this letter to Laodicea is addressed to the whole church. The door on which Christ is knocking is not the door to a single human heart, but the door of the Laodicean church as a whole.

Revelation 3:8, in the letter to the Philadelphians, also uses the image of a door. Jesus says to that church, "See, I have placed before you an open door that no one can shut. I know that you have little strength, yet you have kept my word and have not denied my name." This is another use of "door" as a symbol of opportunity for greater fellowship with God, not of conversion. God has already opened this door, and it always stands open. This is unusual for a literal door, but typical of God's grace and invitation.

What does the misunderstanding of Revelation 3:20 have correct? It accurately sees Jesus as the one knocking on the door. His knocking and his voice summon those inside to respond. But this knocking is not for initial conversion, as the misunderstanding supposes, but for continual conversion. Jesus knocks on the door of a church badly in need of repentance, reform, and rededication. To open the door to Jesus is to welcome him more fully into the church's life, and to come into full and rich fellowship with him. Although Jesus is knocking on the church's door and wants a response from that whole church, it's not simply a group matter. (If your household is like mine, whenever an unexpected knock comes at the front door, family members look at each other to see who will answer it.) Each individual believer has a role in hearing Jesus knock and letting him in.

What is the significance of the corrected understanding for Christians today? First, it's clear from this passage, and from all the letters to the seven churches found in Revelation 2–3, that congregational life can sometimes go very wrong. Churches in ancient times and today can be infected by false doctrine, be divided by relatively unimportant issues, tolerate evils in their midst, and become lukewarm to God. Jesus knocks on the door of our churches to call them to repentance and obedience. This is why the verse immediately before "I stand at the door and knock" shows that Jesus is knocking to "reprove" and "discipline," and that he calls them to "Be earnest and repent" (Revelation 3:19). There is hope for errant churches, because Jesus himself calls them to repent.

Second, life in the church is not in the end a matter of following rules, as important as God's commandments are, but of deeper fellowship with Christ that produces deeper obedience. We need reproof and discipline, but what matters is how Jesus reproves and disciplines us. He doesn't say, "I will enter and keep repeating my commands until you obey them," but "I will enter and eat with you, and you with me." All obedience to God flows from being in right and full relationship with God, and this relationship is a sharing in fellowship with God in the company of others (v. 20) and a sharing in Jesus' power to rule based on "conquering" death by submitting to it (v. 21).

We conclude by returning to the story of William Holman Hunt's painting, *The Light of the World*. When the original painting was given to Keble College of the University of Oxford, the donors wanted to hang it prominently in the college's main chapel, where it could appeal to everyone who entered. It could even be seen by people passing by the entrance to the chapel but didn't want to go in, and the donors thought that this would plant a seed that could lead to their salvation. College officials eventually hung it, for their own reasons, in a smaller side chapel next to the main chapel, where it is still found. Those who want to see it must go into the main chapel, then into the side chapel, and look to the front wall to see it in an honored place above the altar. This placement aligns, not intentionally, with the correct interpretation of Revelation 3:20. Just as the painting of Christ knocking at the door can now be viewed only by those inside the chapel, so too those on the inside of our churches are invited to experience Christ knocking for them.

QUESTIONS FOR REFLECTION AND DISCUSSION

1. What did you understand as the meaning of "Behold I stand at the door and knock," prior to this study?
2. Do you see the church as "a church badly in need of repentance, re-dedication, and reform"? What are the symptoms?
3. What might it look like for the church to open the door to Christ and come into fuller communion?
4. Find photos of these two paintings online, and compare them. What to you are the important similarities and differences?
5. What is your newly expanded understanding of this verse?
6. What does this understanding call the church as a whole, and your congregation, to do?

Bibliography

American Heritage Dictionary of the English Language. 4th ed. Boston: Houghton Mifflin, 2000.
American Psychological Association. *Forgiveness: A Sampling of Research Results.* Washington DC: Office of International Affairs, 2006. https://web.archive.org/web/20110626153005/http:/www.apa.org/international/resources/forgiveness.pdf.
Barth, Karl. *The Epistle to the Romans.* Translated by Edwyn C. Hoskyns. London: Oxford University Press, 1933.
Boer, Roland. "Why I Am a Christian Communist." Taking Notes 24. *Philosophers for Social Change* (blog), July 30, 2013. https://philosophersforchange.org/2013/07/30/taking-notes-24-why-i-am-a-christian-communist/.
Catholic Church. *Catechism of the Catholic Church.* "Respect for Human Life." Part 3, Section 2, Chapter 2, Article 5, Section 1. http://www.vatican.va/archive/ENG0015/__P7Z.HTM/.
Dictionary.com. "Cross to Bear." http://www.dictionary.com/browse/cross-to-bear.
Dunn, James D. G., and John Rogerson, eds. *Eerdmans Commentary on the Bible.* Grand Rapids: Eerdmans, 2003.
Fantz, Ashley. "Outrage over 6-Month Sentence for Brock Turner in Stanford Rape Case." http://www.cnn.com/2016/06/06/us/sexual-assault-brock-turner-stanford/.
Goldingay, John. *The Old Testament for Everyone.* Louisville: Westminster John Knox, 2010–2016.
Hagin, Kenneth E. *Seven Things You Should Know about Divine Healing.* Faith Library. Tulsa: Faith Library Publications, 1979.
Hirsch, E. D., Jr. *Dictionary of Cultural Literacy.* Boston: Houghton Mifflin, 1988.
Kennedy, D. James. *Evangelism Explosion: Equipping Churches for Friendship, Evangelism, Discipleship, and Healthy Growth.* Revised by D. James Kennedy and Thomas H. Stebbins. 4th ed. Wheaton, IL: Tyndale House, 1996.
Kindlon, Dan, and Michael Thompson. *Raising Cain: Protecting the Emotional Life of Boys.* New York: Ballantine, 1999.
Kinnaman, David, and Gabe Lyons. *Unchristian: What a New Generation Really Thinks about Christianity . . . and Why It Matters.* Grand Rapids: Baker, 2007.
Lloyd, Niles. "Jesus Is Knocking." http://www.sermoncentral.com/sermons/jesus-is-knocking-niles-lloyd-sermon-on-salvation-51626.asp?Page=2.
Luther, Martin. *Luther's Small Catechism.* Translated by Timothy J. Wengert. Edited by Jeffrey S. Nelson and Elisabeth Drotning. Minneapolis: Augsburg Fortress, 2001.

Morgan, Robert J. *100 Bible Verses Everyone Should Know by Heart.* Nashville: B & H, 2010.
Murray, David. "Ten Reasons Why the KJV Is Still the Most Popular Version." http://headhearthand.org/blog/2014/03/19/10-reasons-why-the-majority-of-christians-still-read-the-kjv/
Murray, James A. H., et al., eds. *The Oxford English Dictionary.* 13 vols. Oxford: Clarendon, 1933.
Niebuhr, H. Richard. *The Kingdom of God in America.* 1937. Reprinted, New York: Harper & Row, 1959.
Schultz, Richard L. *Out of Context: How to Avoid Misinterpreting the Bible.* Grand Rapids: Baker, 2012.
Singer, Peter. *Animal Liberation.* New York: Avon, 1975.
Smedes, Lewis. *Forgive and Forget: Healing the Hurts We Don't Deserve.* San Francisco: Harper & Row, 1984.
Smith, Joseph Fielding, Jr. *The Way to Perfection.* Salt Lake City: Deseret, 1931.
Spencer, Andrew. "The Importance of Rejecting the Prosperity Gospel." *The Public Square and Theology 101* (blog), January 28, 2014, The Institute for Faith, Work & Economics. https://tifwe.org/the-importance-of-rejecting-the-prosperity-gospel/.
Sprinkle, Preston M. *Fight: A Christian Case for Non-Violence.* Colorado Springs: Cook, 2013.
Stamm, Johann J., and Maurice E. Andrew. *The Ten Commandments in Recent Research.* Studies in Biblical Theology, 2nd ser., 2. London: SCM, 1967.
Walters, Joanna. "Yahoo CEO Marissa Mayer's Minimal Maternity Leave Plan Prompts Dismay." Technology. *Guardian,* September 2, 2015. https://www.theguardian.com/technology/2015/sep/02/yahoo-ceo-marissa-mayer-minimal-maternity-leave-plan-prompts-dismay/.
Waltke, Bruce K. *Finding the Will of God: A Pagan Notion?* 2nd ed. Grand Rapids: Eerdmans, 2016.
Wansbrough, Henry. *The Use and Abuse of the Bible: A Brief History of Biblical Interpretation.* London: T. & T. Clark, 2010.
Westerhoff, John H., III. *Will Our Children Have Faith?* 3rd rev. ed. Harrisburg, PA: Morehouse, 2012.
Wilkin, Robert N., et al. *Four Views on the Role of Works at the Final Judgment.* Counterpoints. Grand Rapids: Zondervan, 2013.
Wilkinson, Bruce. *The Prayer of Jabez: Breaking through to the Blessed Life.* Sisters, OR: Multnomah, 2000.
Willard, Dallas. *The Spirit of the Disciplines: Understanding How God Changes Lives.* San Francisco: Harper & Row, 1988.
Wright, N. T. The New Testament for Everyone. Louisville: Westminster John Knox, 2001–2015.
———. *Surprised by Hope: Rethinking Heaven, the Resurrection, and the Mission of the Church.* New York: HarperOne, 2008.

www.ingramcontent.com/pod-product-compliance
Lightning Source LLC
Chambersburg PA
CBHW022121160426
43197CB00009B/1111